Praise for *The Breaking of Nations*

"By reading Cooper, we can better understand the intellectual and ideological underpinnings of Britain's prime minister, whose decision to support the war in Iraq was as deeply unpopular at home as it was admired in Washington. And we can better understand European security policy." —*The Nation*

"A slender but not slight consideration of Europe's future on a hostile planet." —*Kirkus Reviews*

"Robert Cooper is Europe's preeminent scholar-diplomat. His bold vision for the future of Europe, and of the United States, is full of wisdom and admirable idealism. This brilliantly written book carries the transatlantic conversation to the next stage." —Robert Kagan, author of *Of Paradise and Power*

"Robert Cooper is one of the world's most thoughtful diplomats, and he brings his world of experience to bear on the dilemmas we face after September 11 in a way that any reader will find both readable and illuminating." —Professor Joseph S. Nye, author of *The Paradox of American Power,* dean of the Kennedy School of Government, and former chair of the American National Intelligence Council

"Cooper is a formidable thinker. . . . [He] advances his central argument with verve and sophistication. He shows brilliantly that states, and the people who compose them, can radically change conceptions of both their interests and their identities." —*The Independent*

THE BREAKING OF NATIONS

Order and Chaos in the Twenty-first Century

ROBERT COOPER

GROVE PRESS
New York

First published in Great Britain in 2003 by Atlantic Books, an imprint of Grove Atlantic Ltd.

Printed in the United States of America

Grateful acknowledgement is made to Faber & Faber Limited for permission to reproduce the lines on page 152 from *War Music* by Christopher Logue (London: Faber, 1988).

Sections of this book were published in earlier forms as *The Postmodern State and the World Order* by Demos in 1996; and by Demos and the Foreign Policy Centre in 2000. The publishers gratefully acknowledge the assistance of Demos and the Foreign Policy Centre in the publication of this book.

FIRST GROVE PRESS EDITION

Library of Congress Cataloging-in-Publication Data

Cooper, Robert, 1947–
    The breaking of nations : order and chaos in the twenty-first century / Robert Cooper.
        p. cm.
    Originally published: London : Atlantic Books, 2003.
    Includes bibliographical references and index.
    ISBN 0-8021-4164-1 (pbk.)
    1. International relations. 2. Security, International. 3. Europe—Foreign relations—United States. 4. United States—Foreign relations—Europe.
I. Title.

JZ1308.C664 2004
327.1'01—dc22   2003062984

Grove Press
an imprint of Grove/Atlantic, Inc.
841 Broadway
New York, NY 10003

04 05 06 07 08   10 9 8 7 6 5 4 3 2 1

CONTENTS

ACKNOWLEDGEMENTS

The original version of Part I was published by Demos in 1996. A second updated version was published again by Demos in 1999. I am grateful to Demos (in particular to Geoff Mulgan and Tom Bentley) for stimulating me to write and for the helpful advice they gave along the way.

Part II (which was originally intended to be a short note for the Prime Minister to read at Christmas) developed into a longer essay at the instigation of Mark Leonard and the Foreign Policy Centre. It had originally been my plan to publish it with them. I am grateful for all the help they gave me and also for their willingness to allow me to pursue the project in this altered form.

A shorter version of Part III first appeared in *Internationale Politik* as a farewell present from me to Dr Angelika Volle. I am grateful to her and to *Internationale Politik*.

I have received helpful comments from too many people to recall on all parts of this work but I should particularly mention Heather Grabbe and Alexandras Yannis for whose comments on Part II I am especially grateful. I am also indebted to Carl Hallergard, who drew my attention to the quotation from Nietzsche in Part III, and to the ideas that lie behind it.

Finally, I should thank both the British Government and the General Secretariat of the Council of the European Union, who have generously allowed me to publish over the years in spite of my official position. The ideas in these essays are my own (insofar as anybody can own an idea) and any resemblance to British or European policy is purely accidental.

PREFACE

The worst times in European history were in the fourteenth century, during and after the Hundred Years War, in the seventeenth century at the time of the Thirty Years War, and in the first half of the twentieth century. The twenty-first century may be worse than any of these.

The first two periods were times when order broke down, when church, state and other ties of obligation were losing their power to discipline men's aggression. In the fourteenth century, the old order of chivalry was fading; feudal ties, weakened in endless wars, were giving way to patriotism; and the Church was divided by France's creation of the Avignon Papacy. After the Hundred Years' War, bands of soldiers roamed the ruined landscape of France terrorizing the countryside.

In the seventeenth century, the Church was split by the new Protestant movements and the wars that followed were both wars between states and wars of religion. Bringing together the power of the state and the fanaticism of the faithful, these wars without limit and without mercy laid waste to central Europe. Social order all but collapsed. By some accounts, a third of the population of Germany died. Every ten years in a passion play, the citizens of the Bavarian town of Oberammergau still give thanks for their deliverance from the Swedes. For most countries outside Europe, too, the worst memories of history are of periods of disorder: the era of the warring states in China, for example. Golden ages are usually times of strong government.

The European crisis in the twentieth century showed that the opposite can also be true. The wars of twentieth-century Europe were the first great wars of industrial society, wars of machines as well as men; they were also wars of over-powerful states able to mobilize their societies as never before; and they were made more deadly by nationalism and ideology. In this multiple catastrophe, the single most important thing that went wrong was that technology overran political maturity. Those who started the First World War had expected it to resemble the short wars of their child-hood, not understanding the capacity of an industrial age to deliver men and munitions endlessly to the front. For the remainder of that half-century the machinery of propaganda, control and murder was turned against domestic and foreign populations in Germany, the Soviet Union and elsewhere. Then, for a moment, it seemed as if the nuclear revolution might complete the triumph of technology over mankind; but somehow political wisdom returned and there was a pause in civilization's pursuit of self-destruction.

The new century risks being overrun by both anarchy and technology. The two great destroyers of history may reinforce each other. And there is enough materiel left over from previous centuries in the shape of national, ideological and religious fanaticisms to provide motives for the destruction.

Both the spread of terrorism and that of weapons of mass destruction point to a world in which Western governments are losing control. The spread of the technology of mass destruction represents a potentially massive redistribution of power away from the advanced industrial (and democratic) states towards smaller states that may be less stable and have less of a stake in an orderly world; or, more dramatically still, it may represent a redistribution of power away from the state itself and towards individuals, that is to say terrorists or criminals. If proliferation were to take place in this fashion it would not only be Western governments that would be losing control, but all those people who have an interest in an orderly world.

In the past, to be damaging an ideological movement had to be widespread to recruit enough support to take on authority. Probably there had to be genuine grievances behind it. Henceforth, comparatively small groups will be able to do the sort of damage which before only state armies or major revolutionary movements could achieve. A few fanatics with a 'dirty bomb' (one which sprays out radiological material) or biological weapons will be able to cause death on a scale not previously envisaged. The Japanese cult Aum Shinrikyo's attempt to use anthrax in Tokyo failed, but sooner or later one of their successors will succeed somewhere in the world. A serious terrorist attack could be launched by perhaps sixty people, provided they were sufficiently committed, courageous and competent (or, alternatively, fanatical, foolhardy and fortunate). 0.000001 per cent of the population is enough. Emancipation, diversity, global communication – all the things that promise an age of riches and creativity – could also bring a nightmare in which states lose control of the means of violence and people lose control of their futures. Civilization and order rests on the control of violence: if it becomes uncontrollable there will be no order and no civilization.

The three essays in this collection are indirect reflections from different angles on this situation and on what can be done about it.

The first describes the state of the world and the state of the state, a decade after the end of the Cold War. The most obvious feature of this world is American power; but in the long run the most important facts may be the end of empire and the transformation of the state through globalization. The most hopeful feature is the emergence of the postmodern[1] system of security in Europe. And the most worrying is the encroachment of chaos on the civilized world – from around it and within it. Europe may be able to stop the approach of chaos through the Balkans or even from across the Mediterranean, but it may prove more difficult to deal with chaos in its own suburbs and declining industrial towns.

The descent into chaos will not happen quickly. There is still time to tackle the problems that will cause it. Dealing directly with terrorism and weapons of mass destruction may contain those threats, but it will not end them. The time bought by direct action must be used to solve some of the underlying problems. If states are to retain control, the first condition is that they should make peace with each other so that they can face the common threat of disorder together. A background of peace among states is essential both for a policy of containment and for self-preservation. States weaken and destroy themselves through war. Conflict fuels fanaticism and then gives the fanatics the means of destruction. Without the wars in Afghanistan there would have been no Osama bin Laden.

The second essay is about how to make peace. It begins as a general reflection on diplomacy, but concludes with a view of the conditions for the creation of a postmodern peace. It is written in admiration of the men and women who built the European peace and the transatlantic relationship after the

Second World War, the only example of a lasting peace among nations.

Eventually, the lessons of this success might teach us and others how to spread the peace more widely. The question is whether there will be enough time. Bringing European countries together after centuries of war was a remarkable feat, but it took a catastrophe to achieve it. And it was done against the background of a common history and culture. The most worrying thing about globalization is that it brings us new, more foreign enemies whose motives we barely understand.

It may be that modern science, which gave us the weapons, will also give us the means of controlling them. But history suggests that the solution to the problems of technology is better politics rather than better technology.

The third essay is a comment on Europe today. If we are going to keep out the storm that threatens us in the next decades, we have to harness for good the enormous potential that Europe represents. It will not be enough to leave the world to the United States. The conditions of peace in the twenty-first century are so difficult and the conditions of war so terrible that all must contribute together.

PART ONE
THE CONDITION OF THE WORLD

INTRODUCTION

The year 1989 marks a break in European history. What happened then was more far-reaching than the events of 1789, 1815 or 1919. Those dates stand for revolutions, the break-up of empires and the re-ordering of spheres of influence. But until 1989, change took place within the established framework of the balance of power and the sovereign independent state. Nineteen eighty-nine was different. To the dramatic changes of that year – the revolutions and the re-ordering of alliances – must be added a fundamental change in the European state system itself.

What happened in 1989 was not just the cessation the Cold War, but also the end of the balance-of-power system in Europe. This change is less obvious and less dramatic than the lifting of the Iron Curtain or the fall of the Berlin Wall, but it is deeper and more important. And, in fact, the change in the system is closely associated with both of these events and perhaps was even a precondition for them.

Historically, the best point of comparison is 1648, the end of the Thirty Years War when the modern European state system emerged at the Peace of Westphalia. What has been emerging into the daylight since 1989 is not a rearrangement of the old system but a new system. Behind this lies a new form of statehood, or at least states that are behaving in a radically different way from the past. Alliances that survive in peace as well as in war, interference in each other's domestic affairs and the acceptance of jurisdiction of international courts mean that states today are less absolute in their sovereignty and independence than before.

In a curious symmetry these changes have also come about following a second thirty years' war: 1914 to 1945. The First and Second World Wars brought a level of destruction that Europe had not seen since the first Thirty Years War. In both cases, 1648 and 1945, the result was a recognition that there had been a radical failure and the system was changed. A second important factor was the nuclear confrontation of the Cold War: this offered the possibility of devastation on a scale without historical precedent. At the same time, it froze Europe for forty years. The Cold War and the threat of nuclear confrontation was a reason to put aside the normal quarrels that had bedevilled European politics. The Iron Curtain provided a clear border and led to a stable alliance structure under American leadership. All of this allowed a breathing space for new ideas and new systems to emerge. A change in the state system in Europe was clearly required: if the existing system was producing such unacceptable levels of actual and potential destruction, it was not performing its function. We should not, therefore, be surprised to see a new form of state system emerging.

Thinking about foreign affairs – like any other kind of thinking – requires a conceptual map, which, as maps do, simplifies the landscape and focuses on the main features. Before 1648, the key organizing concept for Europe was the unity of Christendom (the term 'Europe' was hardly used until the late seventeenth century). After the Peace of Westphalia, it was the balance of power. Since 1648 the European order, and the policies that predominated within it, have been given a variety of names: 'the concert of Europe', 'collective security' and 'containment'. Each of these was in fact the name for a variation on the nation state and the balance of power (collective security under the League of Nations was a special and particularly unsuccessful variation). If, as this essay argues, Europe has now moved beyond the balance-of-power system, we need to understand the new system on which our security is based. It requires a new vocabulary and, up to a point, new policies.

A particular problem in understanding the international system – as opposed to the European system – is that it has become less unified since the end of the Cold War.

The Cold War brought the international system together in a global confrontation and seemed to invest even obscure corners of the world with strategic significance. Most foreign policy issues could be viewed in the light of a single overwhelming question: was it good for Us or for Them, for the West or the Soviet Bloc, capitalism or communism? With the end of the Cold War this artificial unity of vision has been lost, and with it perhaps some of the uniting leadership of the United States. Unity has also been lost in another sense. As will be argued later on, while Europe is developing a new and more orderly security system, other parts of the world are becoming more disorderly. It was perhaps natural that with one global order gone, statesmen should want to hail the arrival of a new one, as President Bush did after Gulf War I. But, as is now obvious, this is a poor description of the actual state of affairs.

Understanding the kind of world we live in is important. The costs of intellectual errors in foreign affairs are enormous. Wars are sometimes fought by mistake. Suez was a mistake, at least for Britain: it was fought on the basis that Nasser was a new Hitler and a threat to order, but neither the threat nor the order really existed. Algeria was a mistake: France was fighting for a concept of the state that was no longer sustainable. Vietnam was a mistake: the United States thought it was fighting the Cold War, when in reality it was continuing a French colonial campaign. These conceptual errors had heavy costs. Clarity of thought is a contribution to peace.

The purpose of this essay is to explain the changes that have taken place and to offer a framework for understanding the post-Cold War world. The central focus will be on Europe. It is Europe that has dominated, first actively and then passively, the international stage for about 500 years. It is also in Europe that systemic change has taken place: the nation state balance-of-power system first came into being in Europe; and now the post-balance system of postmodern states has also begun in Europe. But in the age of globalization no continent is an island and the key question for Europe has ceased to be how it can end its fratricidal conflicts and become instead, how it can live in a world where conflicts, missiles and terrorists ignore borders, and where the familiar certainties of the Cold War and its alliances have gone.

1
THE OLD WORLD ORDER

To understand the present we must first understand the past. In a sense, the past is still with us. International order used to be based either on hegemony or on balance. Hegemony came first. In the ancient world, order meant empire: Alexander's Empire, the Roman Empire, the Mogul, Ottoman or Chinese Empires. The choice, for the ancient and medieval worlds, was between empire and chaos. In those days imperialism was not yet a dirty word. Those within the empire had order, culture and civilization. Outside the empire were barbarians, chaos and disorder.

The image of peace and order through a single hegemonic power centre has remained strong ever since. It was first present in late medieval dreams of the restoration of Christendom (by such writers as Dante), or in the many proposals for world or European government made over the years by idealists such as Immanuel Kant, Saint-Simon, Victor Hugo or Andrew Carnegie; it is still visible today in calls for a United States of Europe. The idea of the United Nations as a world government (which it was never intended to be) still survives; and the United Nations is often criticized for failing to be one.

However, it was not the empires but the small states that proved to be a dynamic force in the world. Empires are ill-designed for promoting change. Holding the empire together – and it is the essence of empires that they bring together diverse communities under a single rule – usually requires an authoritarian political style; innovation, especially in society and politics, leads to instability. Thus the standard instructions to a provincial governor in the Chinese Empire were to ensure that nothing changed. Historically speaking, empires have generally been static.

Europe's world leadership came out of that uniquely European contribution, the small state. In Europe, a third way was found between the stasis of chaos and the stasis of empire. In the particular circumstances of medieval Europe, empire had become loose and fragmented. A tangled mass of jurisdictions competed for control: landowners, free cities, holders of feudal rights, guilds and the king. Above all the Church, representing what remained of the Christian empire, still held considerable power and authority, competing with the secular powers.

The success of the small state came from its achievement in establishing a concentration of power – especially the power to make and to enforce the law – at a single point: that is to say in the establishment of sovereignty. Unlike the Church, whose claim was to universal rule, the state's secular authority was limited geographically. Thus Europe changed from a weak system of universal order to a pattern of stronger but geographically limited sovereign authorities without any overall framework of law. The war of all against all that Hobbes feared was prevented by the concentration of legitimate force at a series of single points; but both legitimacy and force were exclusive to single states. Hobbes' primary concern was domestic order; he had lived through the Civil War in England. But the concentration of power at home left the international order without the shelter – admittedly now a very leaky one – that the Church had provided in the shape of a system of law and authority to which even kings were subject. Domestic order was purchased at the price of international anarchy.

The diversity of the small European states created competition. And competition, sometimes in the form of war, was a source of social, political and technological progress. The difficulty of the European state system, however, was that it was threatened on either side. On the one hand, there was the risk of war getting out of control and the system relapsing into chaos. On the other, there was a risk of a single power winning the wars and imposing a single hegemony on Europe.

The solution to this, the essential problem of a small-state system, was the balance of power. This worked neither so perfectly nor so automatically as is sometimes imagined. The idea that the states of Europe would, by some semi-automatic Newtonian process, find an equilibrium among themselves that would prevent any one of them dominating the continent nevertheless retains a powerful grip on the historical imagination. For a hundred years the principle of maintaining a balance of power in the European continent was written into the annual Mutiny Acts of the British Parliament. Nevertheless, whatever the conceptual confusions (to which the US National Security Strategy has just added with its references to a 'balance of power for peace' – which seems to mean the same thing as US dominance), when it came to the point that the European state system was threatened by imperial ambitions from Spain, France or Germany, coalitions were put together to thwart those ambitions. This ran with the grain of the system: a sovereign power is naturally inclined to protect its sovereignty. This system also had a certain legitimacy; statesmen were conscious of the desirability of balance. Over the decades following the Thirty Years War, a consensus grew among governments and elites that the pluralism of

European states should be maintained. Many saw this as a condition of liberty in Europe.

With the balance of power went the doctrine of *raison d'état*. Machiavelli first put forward the proposition that states should not be subject to the same moral constraints as individuals. This philosophy – that moral rules do not apply to states – was the counterpart of the changes by which the state ceased to be the private property of its ruler. At the same time it reflected the breakdown of the Church's universal authority. Acceptance of *raison d'état* grew from the Renaissance onwards until, by the end of the nineteenth century, it was the accepted wisdom and questions that had troubled Aquinas and Augustine about whether or not wars were just were no longer considered relevant.

Nevertheless, the balance of power had an inherent instability. It was the system in which a war was always waiting to happen. The end of the system came about as a result of three factors. The first was German unification in 1871. Here, for the first time, was a state that was too large and too dynamic to be contained within the traditional European system. Restraining German ambitions twice required the intervention of non-traditional European powers: the United States and the Soviet Union. And on the second occasion both remained behind, changing the nature of the system for ever.

The second factor was the change in technology in the late nineteenth century, which brought the Industrial Revolution on to the battlefield. War was inherent in the balance-of-power system: but by the beginning of the twentieth century, technology was raising the price of warfare to unaffordable levels.

The third change came with the second. The Industrial

Revolution brought with it not just the means of moving the masses to the battlefield, but also mass society and democratic politics. This meant that war and peace could no longer be left to the judgement of a small and internationally orientated élite. Balance-of-power thinking could be maintained in the Treaty of Utrecht or the Congress of Vienna or in Bismarck's Treaty with Austria after the war of 1866. But already in 1871 the influence of popular national feeling was playing a part. Bismarck's annexation of Alsace-Lorraine, against his own better judgement, showed that the Bismarckian days, when states could be juggled and balanced, were coming to an end.[2] By the time of the Versailles Conference, the kind of peace negotiations that Talleyrand and Metternich had conducted were no longer possible. The idea of the balance of power was already dead in 1919, although the Second World War saw one final coalition to save the European state system.

If the European state system of the eighteenth and nineteenth centuries (and up to a point the first half of the twentieth century) was one of the balance of power, the world system was one of empires. The empires were, for the most part, the European system writ large. And the wars of empires – for example the Seven Years War – were essentially European wars. Empires added wealth and prestige and provided the background for European politics – whether in the Congress of Berlin or in the Agadir Incident – but the heart of the system still lay in Europe.[3] That European powers had empires overseas was natural given their relative strength and their acquisitiveness, but it was also a paradox. The paradox was that powers which operated a system of balance in their own continent – with its acceptance of national states and international pluralism – operated empires overseas that suppressed nationalism and were hostile to pluralism. This paradox was at the bottom of the unravelling of the empires in the second half of the twentieth century.

But empires were also natural. It is an assumption of the balance-of-power system that states are fundamentally aggressive or at least that some states are aggressive some of the time. A system designed to thwart hegemonic ambitions makes the assumption that such ambitions are common. And, since balance in Europe prevented expansion there, it was natural for that expansion to take place overseas. This is another reason why Germany was a disturbing factor. By the time of Germany's emergence most of the available chaos had already been converted into empire (and some of the non-chaos, too) or had been declared empire-free (South America under the Monroe Doctrine). This left little room for Germany or Japan.

THE COLD WAR ORDER

The wars of 1914 to 1945 destroyed both the European balance of power in its traditional sense and also the European empires. The empires depended on prestige, and this was fatally undermined by the Japanese successes in the Second World War. In Europe itself, America and Russia were now needed to keep the system intact. What happened after 1945 was, however, not so much a radically new system as the concentration and culmination of the old one. The empires became spheres of influence of the superpowers. And the old multilateral balance of power in Europe became a bilateral balance of terror world-wide. In a strange way the old systems – balance in Europe and empire outside – were combined to produce something like a world order of balance between empires or blocs: a final culminating simplification of the balance of power.

The Cold War years were a period of wars and tension, but there was also an underlying order. This came in the shape of a tacit understanding that the United States and the Soviet Union would go to great lengths not to fight each other directly, as would their major allies. Behind this, of course, lay nuclear weapons. The other side of this coin was that the Soviet Union was free to invade its own allies without Western interference. These unwritten rules also permitted the Soviets to arm North Vietnam, and America to arm Afghan guerrillas; but neither sent conventional combat forces to a theatre where the other was committed. For the most part, the Cold War was fought with propaganda, bribery and subversion. Where there was military combat, it was most often for political or ideological control of a particular country – Nicaragua, Angola or Korea, for example – rather than between countries. Many of the actual battles of the Cold War took place in civil wars. Thus the system had a certain orderliness, since boundaries did not often change and major inter-state conflicts were usually outside the Cold War framework.

And yet the Cold War order was not built to last. Although it was stable on a military level it lacked legitimacy as a system. It was not just that many found the balance of terror repugnant – on the whole it was individuals rather than governments who had the moral doubts. Rather, the ideologies of both sides rejected the division of the world into two camps; each claimed a universal validity and a moral authority for their own version of how the world should be. (On the Western side, this was probably truer in

America than in Europe.) In this sense, the Cold War balance differed from the European balance-of-power system, which was accepted by the governments of the day as legitimate and which, in some sense, matched the rationalist spirit of the times. The Cold War system of balance and division never suited the more universalistic, moralistic spirit of the late twentieth century. Moreover, both sides, within certain limits, were always ready to undermine it.

The end of the Cold War has brought not only the rearrangement of the international scene that usually follows hegemonic wars but also domestic change. Since the Cold War was a battle of ideas as much as one between armies, those changes have not been imposed by occupying forces but introduced to willing, if bemused, governments by hordes of MIT-trained economists, management consultants, seminars and programmes of technical assistance (including the aptly named British Know-How Fund). The unique character of the Cold War is also shown by the fact that instead of extracting reparations – a practice which lasted from the Middle Ages to the twentieth century – the victors have instead given aid to help convert the defeated side. Thus are wars of ideas different from wars of territory.

Ideas are not cost-free. They can be dangerous to peace. Democracy, the victorious idea in the Cold War, is a destroyer of empires. To run a democratic state with majority voting requires a strong sense of identity. Democracy entails the definition of a political community. In many cases, this is provided by the idea of the nation. The break-up of the Soviet Union and of Yugoslavia – both in different ways Cold War empires – is a consequence of the victory of Western liberalism and democracy. The wars in those territories are democracy's wars. Liberalism and nationalism can go together today just as they did for eighteenth- and nineteenth-century states emerging from one or another form of imperial rule.

2
THE NEW WORLD ORDER

The point of this compressed historical survey is to make the case that what came to an end in 1989 was not just the Cold War or even, in a formal sense, the Second World War – since the '2+4' Treaty (ending the post-war arrangements for Berlin and Germany) represents a final settlement of that war too. What came to an end in Europe (but perhaps only in Europe) were the political systems of three centuries: the balance of power and the imperial urge. The Cold War brought together the system of balance and empire and made the world a single whole, unified by a single struggle for supremacy and locked in a single balance of terror. But both balance and empire have today ceased to be the ruling concepts in Europe and, as a consequence, the world no longer forms a single political system.

THE PRE-MODERN WORLD

We live now in a divided world, but divided quite differently from the days of the East–West confrontation. First there is a pre-modern world: the pre-state, post-imperial chaos. Examples of this are Somalia, Afghanistan and Liberia. The state no longer fulfils Max Weber's criterion of having the legitimate monopoly on the use of force. This circumstance may come about because the state has in the past abused that monopoly and has lost its legitimacy. In other cases, given the easy availability of conventional weapons today, it may lose the monopoly. The state itself is a fragile structure. Whether in primitive societies which may have less need of it or in complex urban and industrial societies, which have a lower tolerance of disorder, but a more delicate structure of authority, the order provided by the state is vital to society. Too little order brings the risk of chaos; too much order and the state will stop society from functioning – as we have seen in Communist countries. 'The rapier is like a bird,' says the fencing master to his pupil in the film *Scaramouche.* 'Grasp it too loosely and it will fly away, too tight and you will crush it.'4 So it is with the state and civil society.

The examples above are by no means the only cases of degeneration to a pre-modern state. It is early days since the end of the Cold War and more pre-modern states will emerge. Some areas of the former Soviet Union are candidates, most notably Chechnya. All of the world's major drug-producing areas are part of the pre-modern world. In Afghanistan under the Taliban there was no real sovereign authority. It is much the same in up-country Burma or in some parts of South America, where drug barons threaten the state's monopoly on force. No area of the world is without its risky cases.

What is different today is that the imperial urge is dead in the countries most capable of imperialism. Land and natural resources (with the exception of oil) are no longer a source of power for the most technologically advanced countries. Governing people, especially potentially hostile people, is a burden. Nobody wants to pay the costs of saving distant countries from ruin. The pre-modern world belongs, as it were, in a different time zone: here, as in the ancient world, the choice is again between empire or chaos. And today, because none of us sees the point of empires, we have often chosen chaos.

As a result we have, for the first time since the nineteenth century, a *terra nullius.* It may remain so or it may not. The existence of such a zone of chaos is nothing new; but previously such areas, precisely because of their chaos, were isolated from the rest of the world. Not so today when a country without much law and order can still have an international airport.

While such countries no longer stimulate greed, they may excite pity: television pictures can bring their suffering into our homes. And, where the state is too weak to be dangerous, non-state actors might become too strong. If they become too dangerous for the established states to tolerate, it is possible to imagine a defensive imperialism. If non-state actors, notably drug, crime or terrorist syndicates take to using non-state (that is, pre-modern) bases for attacks on the more orderly parts of the world, then the organized states will eventually have to respond. This is what we have seen in Colombia, in Afghanistan and in part in Israel's forays into the Occupied Territories.[5]

RELIGION AND THE RISE OF THE MODERN

Religion is a crucial factor in this story. Most empires are characterized by a strong religious element. Perhaps this is because the societies they have governed have been largely agrarian, with the characteristic agrarian social structure of peasants, soldiers and priests. The eastern empire of Byzantium and the Western Carolingian Empire were Christian. The Ottoman and Mogul Empires were Islamic.

In the Russian Empire, Moscow was conceived as the third Rome and its subjects were identified by religion rather than ethnicity (Orthodoxy being the mainstream). Its successor, the Soviet empire, was founded on a secular faith in scientific socialism. Indonesia under Suharto – something between an empire and a nation state – employed the state ideology of Pancasila, as well as the army, to hold it together. Only China among the great empires seems to have been without an obvious religious element; the Chinese emperor was nevertheless the Son of Heaven and if things went wrong he could lose his mandate.

Colonial empires are somewhat different. The European empires took with them a strong Christian element – missionaries played a significant part in their creation – but Christianity was rarely used to establish the legitimacy of the empire. Colonial empires are in any case a different kind of structure, since the imperial possessions are the possessions of a state rather than a part of it. The two do not together form a single unit of government; that is to say, Britain was never a part of the British Empire.

The nation state, in contrast to an empire, is characteristically secular. Whereas imperial rule is legitimized by the sanction of heaven (the emperor is appointed by God), national government is legitimized in the end by the nation; from below rather than above. For a while, European monarchs borrowed the authority of the Church and claimed divine right; but this position was difficult to sustain over many centuries. Religions are universal and it is hard to explain why God should appoint so many different monarchs for independent sovereign states.

This logic took some time to work its way through Europe, but by the end of the twentieth century government is in practice almost entirely secular. A striking illustration is provided by Turkey where Atatürk, perhaps instinctively understanding the logic of the nation, insisted that the

Turkish state, which he created out of the dissolving Ottoman Empire, should be secular. With the secularized state goes the amoral state of which Machiavelli was the prophet.

Although the legitimacy of emperors has a religious basis, empires are characterized by diversity, including a diversity of religions. Many of the subjects of the Mogul emperors were Hindus; the Russian emperor had Muslims as subjects; and the Ottoman emperor Christians. In the colonial empires (which governed by technical and cultural superiority together with force rather than by legitimacy) religious faith was equally varied.

Empires usually come to an end through military defeat. In the case of colonial empires, the end might also come as a result of changing circumstances in the colonizing country (the case of post-war Britain, for example, or Portugal). When an empire is defeated the most frequent result is break-up. Occasionally, one empire might be replaced by another, as the Russian empire was replaced by the Soviet empire – something similar happened in Indonesia following the Dutch withdrawal. But break-up is more usual. When an empire breaks up the question of identity becomes relevant for the first time. Under an imperial power there is no requirement for its subjects to identify with it; in contrast, a state, which is legitimized from below, requires some degree of identification from its citizens. National identities are usually created by states out of the raw material of history, culture and language. Sometimes they may exist within an empire, where a historic memory survives (as it did in the Baltic States under Soviet rule). Or they may have been fostered by the colonial power – as they were, up to a point, by Britain. But frequently these identities have proved weak in comparison with more deep-rooted (such as tribal) identities.

Where there is no other identification, religion provides a ready-made source of identity: it is fundamental in people's lives and gives them a sense of who they are. It provides a feeling of community. It is natural, therefore, that in the power vacuum left by a retreating empire group loyalties should coalesce around religious beliefs. Hence, the regular occurrence of religious clashes where a retreating or weakening empire leaves a power vacuum.

The story in Europe was somewhat different. Uniquely, the Christian empire of Western Europe divided itself into a spiritual component and a temporal component. The temporal empire ceased to be meaningful in the early Middle Ages, but the spiritual component survived, and while it did so it prevented the emergence of independent sovereign nation states. In theory at least, the Pope had the power and the duty to adjudicate in disputes between states and was their hierarchical superior. The Treaties of Tordesilla and Saragossa, which divided the world between Spain and Portugal, were a late exercise of this role. (Even today, in some European countries, the Papal Nuncio is still given precedence over the diplomatic representatives of other countries.) The wars of religion in Europe were thus the cause rather than the consequence of the break-up of the empire. It was the split in the Christian Church and the wars that followed that finally lost Christendom its legitimizing function. Thereafter, power and legitimacy belonged to the states – and later to the nation states – of Europe.

THE MODERN WORLD

The second part of the world is the modern. Here the

classical state system remains intact. States retain the monopoly of force and may be prepared to use it against each other. If there is order in this part of the system it is because there is a balance of power or because of the presence of hegemonic states which see an interest in maintaining the status quo, as the United States does in the Pacific. The modern world is for the most part orderly, but it remains full of risks. The Persian Gulf, for example, is an area where it has been necessary to think in balance-of-power terms. The Western concept has sometimes been of a balance between Iran and Iraq. Unfortunately, Iraq's emergence as the stronger power following the Iran–Iraq war brought that theory to an end. And (as in Europe in the first half of the century) the United States has been obliged to become the balancing element, if not the permanent guarantor of peace.

An important characteristic of the modern order (which I call 'modern' not because it is new – it is in fact very old-fashioned – but because it is linked to that great engine of modernization, the nation state) is the recognition of state sovereignty and the consequent separation of domestic and foreign affairs, with a prohibition on external interference in the former. This is still a world in which the ultimate guarantor of security is force, a world in which, in theory at least, borders can be changed by force. It is not that, in the modern order, might is right, but that right is not particularly relevant; power and *raison d'état* are the things that matter. In international relations, this is the world of the calculus of interests and forces described by Machiavelli and Clausewitz.

The concepts, values and vocabulary of the modern world still dominate thinking about international relations. Palmerston's classic statement that Britain had no permanent friends or enemies, but that only its interests were eternal is still quoted as though it were a lasting truth of universal application. Theories of international relations are still broadly based on these assumptions. This is clearly true for 'realist' theories, for example those based on the calculus of interests and the balance of power; it is also true for 'idealist' theories – based on the hope that the anarchy of nations can be replaced by the hegemony of a world government or a collective-security system.

The United Nations, as originally conceived, belongs to this universe. It represents an attempt to establish law and order within the modern state system. The UN Charter emphasizes state sovereignty on the one hand and aims to maintain order by force. The veto power is a device to ensure that the UN system does not take on more than it can handle by attacking the interests of the great powers. The United Nations was thus conceived to stabilize the order of states and not to create a fundamentally new order. This is not the whole story since the United Nations has developed since its inception; but in conception the collective-security element of the UN Charter represents an attempt to throw the weight of the international system behind the *status quo*, so that the international community as a whole would become the balancing actor in the balance-of-power system.

Before passing to the third element in the world system, it is worth noting that the modern order contains some continuing problems characteristic of balance-of-power systems. The most notable is the lack of a real balance in many areas of the world. In the Gulf, for instance, we have already seen the consequences of that. But elsewhere there are also powerful states that might under certain circumstances become destabilizing factors. India is one example – is the nuclear balance with Pakistan going to remain stable? China is another – without the US presence in the region would a balance between China and Japan be stable?

None of these is directly threatening at the moment; for the most part they are preoccupied with economic development and with their own internal security and cohesion. That is also one reason why they hate external interference, which is both a challenge to state sovereignty and a threat to internal order. Any of these countries could, if things went badly wrong for them, revert to a pre-modern state.

But it could be equally alarming if things went right for them. The establishment of internal cohesion has often been the prelude to external expansion. So it was for Britain after England and Scotland unified (the Empire was always 'British'); for Japan after 1868; for Germany after 1871. Both China and India, though they are part of the nation state system, have some of the characteristics of empires. Were they to develop the nation state's ability to concentrate loyalty and power they would be very formidable indeed. In fact, the arrival of any cohesive and powerful state in many parts of the world could prove too much for any regional balance-of-power system.

There are many countries that could become too powerful or too aggressive for regional balance. The names mentioned are merely those of the largest regional actors; but we should not become too fixated by size. Internal cohesion and modern (especially nuclear) technology can compensate for small size as, historically, the case of Britain demonstrates. In the pre-modern world, states (or rather would-be states) may be dangerous because they are failures. In the modern world, it is the successful states that are potentially dangerous.

If powerful new states emerge it is possible that we shall see a new imperialism. Someone may decide to make some part of the chaos a non-white man's burden. If they do so, it will probably not be for economic reasons; taming chaos is not very profitable today – perhaps it never has been. Imperialism is more likely from defensive motives – when a nearby state of chaos becomes in some way a threat. Or imperialism might be in pursuit of an idea. To persuade your own people to risk their lives in chaotic foreign countries requires the belief that you are spreading some gospel, pursuing a mission of civilization or (in the worst case) establishing the natural superiority of your race. It requires confidence and conviction. And then, if you are to be successful, you have to persuade the people that you are subjugating that you are doing this in their own interests and in the service of a higher good; most people are subjugated by ideas rather than by force. In this context, Islam is at least a possibility. A successful Islamist state, fired with enthusiasm for bringing the teachings of the Koran to unbelievers, is more likely to be a threat (or a saviour) for the pre-modern world than sceptical Europeans or a tough-minded, realistic United States.

The conditions for the success of such a new imperialism are much more difficult today than in previous centuries. The new imperialists would encounter a national consciousness awakened (or created) by previous generations of imperialists. They would also have to explain why the idea they offer is superior to the liberal/capitalist/consumerist democracy of the West. These are difficult challenges for a country aiming to establish a new empire; they might well make it impossible to sustain one.

A new imperialism from any of the modern states would

not necessarily be damaging for Western interests since it would be established in a zone that the West had chosen to abandon. More problematic would be the attempt to establish a regional hegemony. This might in the short run be threatening to Western interests and in the long run be threatening to the West itself. We have already seen such a threat in the Gulf with Saddam Hussein's abortive attempt to take over Kuwait; and it is possible to imagine threats arising in the Pacific. If they did, in some years' time, will the West be equipped materially, psychologically and politically to deal with them? That brings us to the problem of postmodernity.

THE POSTMODERN WORLD

The third part of the international system may be called the postmodern element.[6] Here the state system of the modern world is also collapsing, but unlike the pre-modern it is collapsing into greater order rather than disorder. Modern Europe was born with the Peace of Westphalia. Postmodern Europe begins with two treaties. The first of these, the Treaty of Rome (1957), was created out of the failures of the modern system: the balance of power which ceased to balance and the nation state which took nationalism to destructive extremes. The Treaty of Rome is a conscious and successful attempt to go beyond the nation state.

The second foundation of the postmodern era is the Treaty on Conventional Forces in Europe (the CFE Treaty): this was born of the failures, wastes and absurdities of the Cold War. In aspiration at least the Organization for Security and Co-operation in Europe (OSCE) also belongs to this world. So, in different ways, do the Chemical Weapons

Convention (CWC), the Ottawa Convention banning anti-personnel mines and the treaty establishing an International Criminal Court.

The postmodern system does not rely on balance; nor does it emphasize sovereignty or the separation of domestic and foreign affairs. The European Union is a highly developed system for mutual interference in each other's domestic affairs, right down to beer and sausages. The CFE Treaty also breaks new ground in intrusion in areas normally within state sovereignty. Parties to the treaty – essentially the then membership of NATO and the Warsaw Pact – have to notify the location of their heavy weapons (which are in any case limited by the treaty) and allow challenge inspections. Under this treaty, more than 50,000 items of heavy military equipment – tanks, artillery, helicopters and so on – have been destroyed by mutual agreement, surely an unprecedented event. The legitimate monopoly on force that is the essence of statehood is thus subject to international – but self-imposed – constraints.

It is important to realize what an extraordinary revolution this is. The normal, logical behaviour of armed forces is to conceal their strength and hide their equipment from potential enemies. Treaties to regulate such matters are an absurdity in strategic logic. In the first place, you do not reach agreements with enemies since, if they are enemies, they cannot be trusted. In the second place, you do not let the enemy come snooping around your bases counting weapons. The CFE Treaty does precisely that. What is it that has brought about this weird behaviour? The answer must be that behind the paradox of the CFE Treaty lies the equal and opposite paradox of the nuclear age: that in order to defend yourself you had to be prepared to destroy yourself. The shared interest of European countries in avoiding a nuclear catastrophe has proved enough to overcome the normal strategic logic of distrust and concealment. The mutual vulnerability that provided stability in the nuclear age has now been extended to the conventional end of the spectrum where it becomes mutual transparency. (The Cold War nuclear stalemate already contained some elements of the postmodern since it relied on transparency. For deterrence to work it has to be visible.)

The path towards the CFE Treaty was laid through one of the few real innovations in diplomacy – confidence-building measures. Through the fog of mistrust and deception, the Cold War states began to understand late in the day that their ideological opponent might not, in fact, be planning to attack them. Measures to prevent war through miscalculation grew out of this, for example, observation of manoeuvres. These grew eventually into observation of weapons systems and to limitations on them. The solution to the prisoners' dilemma lies in ending mutual secrecy.[7]

In one respect, the CFE Treaty collapsed at an early stage under its own contradictions. As originally designed, it embodied the idea of balance between two opposing blocs. The underlying assumption was one of enmity: balance was required to make it unlikely that either side would take the risk of making an attack. Transparency was required to make sure that there was really a balance. But by the time balance and transparency have been achieved, it is difficult to retain enmity. The result is that transparency remains, but enmity and balance (and one of the blocs) have effectively gone. This was not, of course, the work of the CFE Treaty alone, but of the political revolution that made the treaty possible. It does suggest, however, that there is a basic incompatibility between the two systems: the modern based on balance and the postmodern based on openness do not co-exist well together.

Intrusive verification – which is at the heart of the CFE system – is a key element in a postmodern order where state sovereignty is no longer seen as an absolute. But far-reaching as they might be, arms control treaties such as the CFE Treaty and the CWC are only partial approaches towards a postmodern order.

Although their acceptance of intrusive verification breaks with the absolutist tradition of state sovereignty, the field in which sovereignty has been sacrificed is limited to foreign affairs and security. Thus what is permitted is interference in the domestic aspect of foreign affairs.

The aspirations of the Organization for Security and Co-operation in Europe go rather further. OSCE principles cover standards of domestic behaviour – democratic procedures, treatment of minorities, freedom of the press – which are distant from the traditional concerns of foreign and security policy. Whether the OSCE will develop – as it aspires to – into a system for international monitoring of domestic behaviour remains to be seen. If it does, this will be a further break with the tradition of sovereignty in the European state system, which will take all the OSCE countries (or all those who play by the rules) decisively into a postmodern world.

The characteristics of this world are that within it the distinction between domestic and foreign affairs begins to break down. Is the management of the EU single market domestic or foreign business? The answer is that it is both. Mutual interference in some areas of domestic affairs and mutual surveillance (of food safety, of state subsidies, of budget deficits) is normal for postmodern states. Within the

European Union mergers and subsidies are subject to common rules. In most European countries the judgements of the European Court of Human Rights on all kinds of domestic matters (whether you can beat your children for example) are accepted as final. Force is rejected as a way of settling disputes. Minor disputes might be settled by common rules or court decisions; more fundamental matters, such as the British–Spanish dispute over Gibraltar, are left to time and negotiation. For the most part the rules in the system are self-enforced. No one compels states to obey the rules of the CFE Treaty or to pay fines imposed on them by the European Court of Justice. They do so because of their interest as individual states in making the collective system work and, within the European Union, because all have an interest in maintaining the rule of EU law.

Borders are increasingly irrelevant for postmodern states. Thanks to the missile, the motor car and the satellite, this is a fact of life in the twenty-first century. Within most of the European Union border signs have been removed and you know you are in a different country only by the different colours of the road signs. Legal judgements are now enforced across state borders, right down to parking fines. In this environment security, which was once based on walls, is now based on openness and transparency and mutual vulnerability. In some postmodern relationships – for example, with Russia – transparency is limited and carefully defined in treaties, such as the CFE Treaty. This is a revolution in strategic affairs. Among others the wider application of postmodern principles has brought a revolution in the life of the state.

The most prominent postmodern institutions have already been mentioned, but this list is by no means exclusive.

The Strasbourg Court of Human Rights belongs in this category: it interferes directly in domestic jurisdiction. No less striking is the Convention on Torture, which permits challenge inspection of prisons: inspection visits without warning and without visas, anytime, anywhere. In the economic sphere, the International Monetary Fund (IMF) and the Organization for Economic Co-operation and Development (OECD) operate systems of economic surveillance. The Non-Proliferation Treaty (NPT), taken together with the International Atomic Energy Agency (IAEA) safeguards and special inspection regimes, is also a part of postmodern security – the IAEA additional protocol permits access to any site at any time by nuclear inspectors. The lack of openness on the part of the nuclear powers themselves, not to mention NPT states such as India, Pakistan and Israel, leaves the system incomplete for the moment.

The International Criminal Court is a striking example of the postmodern breakdown of the distinction between domestic and foreign affairs. If the world is going to be governed by law rather than force then those who break the law will be treated as criminals. Thus, in the postmodern world, *raison d'état* and the amorality of Machiavelli have been replaced by a moral consciousness that applies to international relations as well as to domestic affairs: hence also the renewed interest in the question of whether or not wars should be considered just. These institutions have been established by conventional treaties between sovereign states and ratified by national parliaments, but the result is a growing web of institutions that go beyond the traditional norms of international diplomacy.

The new security system of the postmodern world deals with the problems identified earlier that made the balance of power unworkable. By aiming to avoid war it takes account of the horrors of war that modern technology represents; indeed, it depends to a degree on the technology and on the fear of the horrors. It is also more compatible with democratic societies: the open society domestically is reflected in a more open international order. And finally, since security no longer depends on balance, it is able to incorporate large and potentially powerful states. The peaceful reunification of Germany is in itself a proof that the system has changed.

A difficulty for the postmodern state is that democracy and democratic institutions are firmly wedded to the territorial state. The package of national identity, national territory, a national army, a national economy and national democratic institutions has been immensely successful. Economy, law-making and defence may be increasingly embedded in international frameworks and the borders of territory might be less important, but identity and democratic institutions remain stubbornly national. This is the reason why traditional states will remain the fundamental unit of international relations for the foreseeable future, even though they might have ceased to behave in traditional ways.

What is the origin of this change? The fundamental point is that 'the world's grown honest'. A large number of the most powerful states no longer want to fight or to conquer. This gives rise both to the pre-modern and to the postmodern world. France no longer thinks of invading Germany or Italy, although it has nuclear weapons, which should theoretically put it in a position of overwhelming superiority. Nor does it think of invading Algeria to restore order. The imperial instinct is dead, at least among the Western powers. (Though, as we shall see later, imperialism might be returning in new forms.) Acquiring territory is no longer of interest. Acquiring subject populations would for most states be a nightmare.

This is not altogether a novelty. Imperialism has been dying slowly for a long time. Britain was inventing dominion status in the nineteenth century and – admittedly under intense pressure – was letting Ireland go in the early twentieth. Sweden acquiesced in Norwegian independence in 1905. What is completely new, however, is that Europe should consist more or less entirely of states that are no longer governed by the territorial imperative.

If this view is correct, it follows that we should not think of the European Union or even NATO as the reason for half a century of peace in Western Europe; at least not in the crude way that this is sometimes argued – that states which merge their steel and coal industries cannot fight each other, since the raw material of war is commonly owned. Nor does the existence of joint military planning or joint headquarters in the NATO framework mean that war is impossible. Joint institutions do not lead automatically to peace. Nor are they even necessary. After all, the EFTA (European Free Trade Association) countries did not fight each other, even though for a long time most were members of neither NATO nor the European Union. If countries want to fight each other they will find a way. Yugoslavia has shown that a single market and a single currency and integrated armed forces can be broken up if those concerned want to fight.

NATO and the European Union have, nevertheless, played an important role in reinforcing and sustaining the basic fact that Western European countries no longer want to fight each other. NATO has promoted a greater degree of military openness than has ever existed before. Force planning is done in the open, even if it is not quite as much of a joint procedure as it is supposed to be. Joint exercises and an integrated command structure reinforce this openness. Thus within Western Europe there has been, informally, a kind of internal CFE Treaty for many years – since everyone knew exactly what armaments their neighbours had. With the difference that most of the time states were urging each other to increase rather than to cut defence spending.

No doubt the solidarity created by having a common enemy also played a part, at least initially. More imporant was the existence of a common friend. The presence of US forces enabled Germany to keep forces at lower levels than its strategic position would have warranted: without them Germany would have needed to maintain forces large enough to deal with a war on two fronts – against France and Russia simultaneously. Such forces would always be a cause of alarm to both its neighbours and would probably have provoked an arms race as well. This situation, sometimes called the strategic dilemma, is typical of the balance-of-power system. The defensive forces of one country are seen by its neighbours as a threat. If everyone supposes the worst, an arms race or some other form of instability is the result. Such is the logic of the balance of power. The same reasoning would have applied in the nuclear sphere too. As it was, the US nuclear guarantee enabled Germany to remain non-nuclear. But even if Germany had pursued a policy of a low level of armaments and had chosen to remain non-nuclear this would not have been enough, at least not if these policies had been followed in isolation. France or Britain might still have suspected a secret German troop build-up or a secret nuclear weapons programme. What mattered above all therefore was the openness NATO created. NATO was and is a massive intra-Western confidence-building measure.

This is why the reunification of Germany within NATO was so important. In a curious way, it is part of how NATO won the Cold War: not by beating Russia, but by changing the strategic position of Germany. NATO provided a framework within which Germany – the epicentre of the Cold War – could be reunited. The balance-of-power system broke down in Europe because of Germany and, for a while, it seemed that the solution to the problem was to divide Germany (just as it had been after the Thirty Years War). And, by the same logic, the Cold War was needed to maintain the division. Balance in Europe required a divided Germany and a divided Germany required a divided Europe. For Germany to be reunited, a different security system was required: in effect a post-balance, postmodern system, of which NATO is one key element.

A united Europe was the other: the European Union's security role is similar to that of NATO, though this is harder to see since it is further from the sharp end of military hardware. It is not the Coal and Steel Authority (which did not integrate the industry so much as the market – German coalmines remained German and French steel mills remained French) that has kept the countries of Europe from fighting each other, but the fact that they did not want to do so. Nevertheless, the Coal and Steel Authority, the Common Market, the Common Foreign and Security Policy and the Common Agricultural Policy (and so forth), have performed important reinforcing functions. They have introduced a new degree of openness hitherto unknown in Europe. And they have given rise to thousands of meetings of ministers and officials, so that all those concerned with decisions over peace and war know each other well.

They may or may not agree; they may or may not like each other, but they do belong to the same organization and work together and make deals together over a wide and wonderful range of subjects: from the conditions under which battery hens are kept to the size of their budget deficits. By the standards of the past this represents an enormous degree of what might be called administrative integration. (This is neither complete political integration – which would require, *inter alia*, European political parties – nor economic integration, which takes place at the level of the firm, the investor and the workforce.) Compared with the past, it represents a quality of political relations and a stability in political relationships never known before. To create an international society, international socialization is required and one of the important functions of the Brussels institutions is to provide this.

A second important function is to provide a framework for settling disputes between member states. Since force is no longer an option, some mixture of law, bargaining and arbitration is required: the European Union provides this in most cases (not all, since, for example, territorial disputes remain outside its ambit). The same framework of bargaining and law also regulates a good deal of transnational co-operation. As one (disappointed) observer noted, the European Union is an organization not for pursuing a European interest, but for pursuing national interests more effectively. In the postmodern context 'more effectively' means without being obliged to resort to military means.

The European Union is the most developed example

of a postmodern system. It represents security through transparency and transparency through interdependence. It is more a transnational than a supranational system. Although there are still some who dream of a European state (which would be supranational), they are a minority today – if one takes account of non-élite opinion, a very small minority. The dream is one left over from a previous age. It rests on the assumption that nation states are fundamentally dangerous and that the only way to tame the anarchy of nations is to impose hegemony on them. It is curious that having created a structure that has transformed the nation state into something more civilized and better adapted to today's world, there are still enthusiasts who want to replace it with something more old-fashioned. If the nation state is a problem, then the super-state is certainly not a solution.

Nevertheless it is unlikely that the European Union, as it is at the start of the twenty-first century, has reached its final resting place. For the long run the most important question is whether integration can remain a largely apolitical process. It is striking that monetary integration has been achieved precisely by removing monetary policy from the hands of politicians and handing it over to the technocrats. This may be no bad thing but, in the deeply democratic culture of Europe, the development of the European Union as a continuation of diplomacy by other means rather than the continuation of politics by other means may in the end exact a price. International institutions need the loyalty of citizens just as state institutions do; and that can be achieved only by giving the citizen some more direct involvement in their management.

*

STATE INTERESTS

To say that the European Union (or for that matter the Council of Europe or the OSCE) is a forum in which states pursue their interests should not be misunderstood. 'Interests' means something different for the modern state and for its postmodern successor. The 'interests' that Palmerston referred to as eternal were essentially security interests. They included notions such as that the Russians should be kept out of the Mediterranean; that no single power should be allowed to dominate the continent of Europe; that the British Navy should be bigger than the next two largest navies combined and so forth. Even defined in these terms, interests are by no means eternal, though they can have a shelf-life measurable in decades at least. These interests are defined by the security problems in a world of fundamentally predatory states. It is the essential business of a state to protect its citizens from invasion: hence the absolute, if not eternal, nature of these interests. Security is, after all, a matter of life and death – which is why they are referred to as 'vital interests'.

Such interests still exist for the West today: for example, it is a vital Western interest that no single country should come to dominate world oil supplies, that nuclear weapons should not get into the hands of unstable, aggressive or irresponsible people, or that terrorist networks should never again be allowed to grow to the dimensions of al-Qaeda. If Japan, for example, should come under serious military threat, there would be a Western interest, probably a vital interest, in defending it. This is because Japanese industry is an integrated component of the global market, vital for many Western manufacturers and retailers, and because a failure to defend a fellow industrial democracy would signal the beginning of the end for all of us.

These are examples of the problems that flow from encounters between the postmodern and the modern world. Within the postmodern world there are no security threats in the traditional sense, because its members do not consider invading each other. The interests that are debated within the European Union are essentially matters of policy preference and burden sharing. There is no fundamental reason why in trade negotiations France should be ready to sacrifice the interests of its software companies in favour of its farmers. This is just a matter of the policy preferences and political affiliations of those who happen to be in power at the time. France's 'interests' are defined by political processes and may change with governments. In Britain, the Thatcher government brought with it a stronger commitment to open markets than its predecessors had shown. The 'interest' in free markets was born in 1979 – it was certainly not eternal. The vital national interests that are defended under the Luxembourg compromise (the mechanism by which some EU states reserve the possibility of exercising a veto when vital interests are at stake) are almost certainly neither vital nor national and they are not even 'interests' in the Palmerstonian sense – none of which is to say that they are unimportant.

If the second half of Palmerston's proposition, that interests are eternal, no longer applies in the postmodern world, the first half, that no country has permanent friends, is equally alien. Although friendship is hardly a concept that applies between states, institutions like the European Union and NATO constitute something analogous to a bond of marriage. In a world where nothing is absolute, permanent or irreversible, the relationships among the postmodern are at least more lasting than any state's interests. Perhaps they will even turn out to be genuinely permanent. Indeed, if they do not then the postmodern experiment will probably have failed.

At all events we should beware of transferring the vocabulary of the modern world into the postmodern. Germany may (occasionally) exercise a dominant influence in the European Union or the USA may dominate NATO policy-making, but this kind of dominance, achieved by persuasion or bought in some other way, is quite different from domination by military invasion. (These two countries are not, of course, mentioned by accident – but the significant fact in each case is probably not their size, but the fact that they are the biggest financial contributors to these two institutions.)

WHO BELONGS TO THE POSTMODERN WORLD?

That there is a new European order based on openness and mutual interference is clear. The EU countries are evidently members; those on its expanding edges perhaps a little more nervously. Whatever happens to the European Union – whether it goes on to become some fuller kind of federation or gets stuck halfway – the state in Western Europe will never be the same again.

Although these postmodern characteristics apply among the states of the European Union they do not necessarily apply between them and other states: when Argentina chose to operate according to the rules of Clausewitz rather than those of Kant, Britain had to respond on the same level. Similarly, during the Cold War, all the European states had to operate on the old logic of power, deception and distrust with regard to the Warsaw Pact, although among themselves the postmodern logic increasingly applied.

Russia poses an important problem. Is it going to be a pre-modern, modern or postmodern state? It embodies all three possibilities. A collapse into pre-modernism is perhaps the least likely; the urbanized and industrialized landscape of Russia has a low tolerance for disorder. The risk is more of the state becoming too powerful than of it disappearing altogether. But there are also postmodern elements in Russia trying to get out. And Russian acceptance of the CFE Treaty and of OSCE observers in Chechnya during the first Chechen war (although not during the second) suggests that it is not wholly lost to the doctrine of openness. How Russia behaves in respect of its postmodern treaty commitments – notably those in the CFE Treaty, but also those it is acquiring through membership of the Council of Europe – will be a critical factor for the future; so will the behaviour of the rest of Europe as it decides how to build its security relationship with Russia.

Of non-European countries, Japan is by inclination a postmodern state. It has self-imposed limits on defence spending and capabilities. It is no longer interested in acquiring territory nor in using force. It would probably be willing to accept intrusive verification. It is an enthusiastic multilateralist. Were it not on the other side of the world, it would be a natural member of organizations such as the OSCE or the European Union. Unfortunately for Japan it is a postmodern country surrounded by states firmly locked into an earlier age: postmodernism in one country is possible only up to a point and only because its security treaty with the US enables it to live as though its neighbourhood were less threatening. If China develops in an unpromising fashion (either modern or pre-modern), Japan could be forced to revert to defensive modernism.

And elsewhere? What in Europe has become a reality is in many other parts of the world an aspiration. ASEAN,[8] NAFTA,[9] MERCOSUR[10] and even the AU,[11] suggest at least an aspiration towards a postmodern environment. Many of these organizations have programmes that follow the pattern developed in the European Union. The postmodern aspiration for a law-governed region is unlikely to be realized quickly. Most developing countries are too jealous of their hard-won independence and too unsure of their own identity to allow much interference in domestic affairs. Nevertheless, imitation is easier than invention and perhaps rapid postmodernization could follow the rapid industrialization that is already under way in many parts of the world. Europe's military power may have declined but the power of example remains. Perhaps that is one postmodern equivalent of imperialism.

THE HEGEMONY OF THE POSTMODERN?

The postmodern group is a powerful and growing collection of states. If we add to that the would-be postmodern Japan and the aspirant countries of Latin America it is a group which should be capable of exerting a strong influence on the way the world is organized, at least in economic terms. Even those who insist on sovereignty find themselves enmeshed in a range of co-operative institutions and agreements governing trade, transport, communications and so on. Sometimes – in order to gain access to financial markets – they may find themselves having to accept interference in their economic affairs from the IMF. Those who want trade agreements with the European Union find that there is a human rights clause attached.

The strongest of the modern states resist this. China has accepted relatively few binding international commitments. India is notoriously resistant to arrangements that might infringe her sovereignty. But most go along with – and all profit from – the multilateral organization of the world.

The multilateral system that has grown up in the post-war world could be seen as the hegemony of the postmodern. In fact it hardly runs so deep. Those parts of the system managed by the World Trade Organization (WTO) and the IMF are vital to prosperity but, unlike the key treaties in Europe, they are not essential to security. For most non-European states the co-operative world system, though highly beneficial to them in many ways, is resented because it interferes with the full exercise of their sovereignty. In a security crisis, where state sovereignty was under real threat, the multilateral links would place little constraint on violent action; at worse they would simply be blown away.

Thus the image of domestic order and international anarchy is false on one level. The world is in fact a highly structured and orderly system (though without a central authority). On the other hand, anarchy remains the underlying reality in the security field for most parts of the world. When someone has decided to use force, the system returns to the law of the jungle, however many trade agreements there may be. This is what happened in Europe with the coming of the First World War, despite the open markets and the high levels of economic interdependence between European states at the time.

In contrast, the co-operative structures in Europe reinforce sovereignty by reinforcing security. If the postmodern system protects your security better than the balance of power did, then it strengthens your ability to exercise your sovereignty.

The point is that European states now define sovereignty differently from hitherto: the state monopoly on law-making no longer exists as far as EU members are concerned; and even for other European countries it is limited by treaties such as those in the Council of Europe framework (e.g. on the jurisdiction of the Court of Human Rights in Strasbourg). The state monopoly on force is also constrained by alliances, by the CFE and other arms control treaties. In some cases, the monopoly on force has been modified by EU agreements about policing (police are the domestic arm of the monopoly of legitimate force), permitting police to operate in limited ways in each other's territory. All of this means that the state of the olden days, sovereign master on its own territory, able to do what it chose when it chose without any kind of outside interference has undergone substantial modification. What in these circumstances does sovereignty amount to for the postmodern state? The answer is probably a mixture of elements: at its core remains domestic control, especially the legal monopoly on force, the ability to make and enforce laws, but internationally the emphasis has shifted from the control of territory and armies to the capacity to join international bodies and to make international agreements. Making peace is as much a part of sovereignty as making war. For the postmodern state, sovereignty is a seat at the table.

THE UNITED STATES

Where does America belong in this world? It would not be too much to say that America invented it. If Europeans have been able to develop security through transparency it is because at the back of this there stands America – and security through armed force. In a sense the United States has stood outside the system, and above it as its guardian.

The central fact of geopolitics today is US military power. America accounts for 38 per cent of all military expenditure in the world and a much higher proportion of military capabilities. There is no conventional force in the world that could fight an all-out war against America and win. Indeed, to put it in wholly unrealistic terms, were all the rest of the world to mount a combined attack on the United States they would be defeated.

Questions about how the world is organized are at least partly questions about US policy. The United States is the only power with a global strategy – in some sense it is the only power with an independent strategy at all. The rest of the world reacts to America, fears America, lives under American protection, envies, resents, plots against, depends on America. Every other country defines its strategy in relation to the United States.

America's aim, like everyone else, is to preserve its national security. Sometimes commentators refer, slightly incredulously, to America's wish to be invulnerable – and indicate with a tinge of European superiority that Europeans, being more experienced, have got used to living with risk over the years. But, were it attainable, being invulnerable is precisely the security policy every country would want. And over the years, out of their geographical good fortune, Americans have indeed become used to invulnerability and are unwilling to compromise on their national security.

Since there is no conventional force in the world that could fight a successful war against the United States, the threats that concern it are both above and below the range of conventional warfare: on the one hand, weapons of mass destruction (WMD); on the other, terrorism. Against WMD held by states deterrence can still provide some protection. Even so, the spread of such weapons remains dangerous and potentially life-threatening, for the United States as well as other countries. First, deterrence cuts both ways. Countries with WMD would achieve a degree of invulnerability *vis-à-vis* the United States – especially if they had nuclear weapons and the means to deliver them on New York. That means that a part of the world, possibly a hostile one, would escape US control; and therein lie many potential dangers. Second, the wider such weapons spread the greater the chance of terrorist groups getting their hands on them. It seems unlikely that deterrence could ever apply to people who have no fixed address and are prepared to die for their cause.

Hence the twin security focus of the United States: the war on terrorism and the campaign to prevent the proliferation of WMD. Those who support and assist the United States in this will gain its protection. Those who seek WMD for themselves or who help terrorists are its enemies. Given the opportunity they will be subject to 'regime change' to a government that has no ambitions for WMD or which is friendly to the United States, preferably both.

In the categories of this essay that makes America a robustly modern state. It is in any case clear that neither the US government nor Congress accepts the necessity or the desirability of interdependence, nor its corollaries of openness, mutual surveillance and mutual interference to the extent that most European governments now do. The United States' unwillingness to accept the jurisdiction of the International Criminal Court and its relative reluctance concerning challenge inspections in the CWC are examples of US caution about postmodern concepts. Since it is the guarantor of the whole system, this is perhaps just as well for the time being.

Besides, as the most powerful country in the world, the United States has no reason to fear any other country and therefore has less reason to accept the idea of security based on mutual vulnerability, except of course in the nuclear field. Here the United States is unavoidably vulnerable. Hence, one very emphatic piece of postmodern diplomacy in an otherwise rather uncompromising insistence on sovereignty: START[12] and all the other nuclear treaties with Russia. At one time one could have pointed to the ABM[13] Treaty, which is designed to preserve mutual vulnerability as the centre-piece of this nuclear postmodernism. The fact that it has gone is an expression of US concerns about emerging threats rather than the mark of a change in its relationship with Russia.

In keeping with its modernist vocation America's approach to international relations is framed by the use of force and by military alliances. In spite of the vast amount of trade and investment that flows across both oceans, the bedrock of the United States' relationships with Europe and Japan is military: NATO and the Security Treaty with Japan.

Is America an imperial power? Not in the usual sense of seeking territory abroad. For much of its history the United States has been consciously anti-imperial, from its own struggle for colonial liberation through to the Monroe doctrine. True, it has interfered relentlessly in Central America, acquired territory by force (as well as purchase) and it was caught up in the imperial frenzy at the end of the nineteenth century; but it was also one of the first to give up its colonies. It then did its best to ensure that the British and French empires were dismantled. The United States is a state founded on ideas and its vocation is the spread of those ideas. European countries are based on nation and history. For Americans history is bunk. They aim, as the Mexican author Octavio Paz says, at the colonization not of space but of time: that is, of the future.

Although the United States has more troops deployed abroad than Britain at the height of its imperial glory, they are not used for the same purpose. Typically, they are there to defend America's allies – Germany during the Cold War, South Korea, Japan and Saudi Arabia (until the removal of Saddam Hussein). An alternative – geopolitical – way of looking at this is to say that US forces are deployed as an outer defensive ring on the periphery of the Eurasian landmass: a rather distant form of forward defence. In most cases they stay in barracks and do little to interfere in the running of the country. Usually they arrive at a time of conflict, but stay on to ensure security and perhaps to strengthen the forces for good government – the two are sometimes related – thereafter. This often turns out to be a long business.

If America is not imperial in the usual sense it is certainly hegemonic: it does not want to rule, but it does aim to control foreign policy. The hegemony is essentially voluntary, part of a bargain in which America provides protection and allies offer bases and support. From an American point of view, countries can choose to be allies or they can be irrelevant, in which case they can be left alone. If they begin to be a threat then they become, potentially at least, a target.

In one respect, however, the United States diverges from the norm of the modern state. There is an imperial tinge to American policy in its desire to promote democracy. This is a cause that attracts both Left and Right, Wilsonians and neo-conservatives. And yet if this is imperial it is also anti-imperial: on the one hand, it tells countries how they should be run; on the other, it tells them they should do the running themselves. It is a typically postmodern approach but it may also have solid modern motivations. On the one hand, it is diametrically opposed to the modern logic of 'He might be a sonovabitch but he's our sonovabitch'; but on the other, there is probably some convergence between making the world safe for democracy and making it safe for America. Like parallel lines, in America the modern and the postmodern may eventually meet.

Pax Romana was an empire, its borders guarded by increasingly forgotten legions. Pax Britannica was an empire also, joined by seas that the British Navy patrolled. But neither was worldwide. In the age of globalization, any sort of Pax Americana has to cover the globe. It cannot do that: even America is not strong enough to manage the whole globe on its own. A global American hegemony is therefore not going to be peaceful, but will be interrupted from time to time by conflicts when a new threat or potential threat is identified. A global alliance, perhaps, but not a global empire: Sparta rather than Athens.

Finally, it is always wise in thinking about America to remember that it is at least as unpredictable as any other country. This is, after all, the country that twice in the twentieth century elected a president on an anti-war ticket, who then took them into a world war; the country that, having declared Korea outside its security perimeter, fought a war there; the country that, following this experience, determined it would never again fight a war on the Asian continent, but then proceeded to do so in Vietnam; and the country that surprised the world by a sudden and fundamental reversal of policy when Nixon visited China (and shortly afterwards abandoned the fixed dollar parity). Today we find an administration, that arrived in office rejecting 'nation building', engaged in a great nation-building project in Iraq. Domestically, too, there have been sharp swings of mood: prohibition, isolationism, McCarthyism and later the anti-war movement all provide illustrations. In this perhaps the United States is no different from any other country – except that with its immense power, changes in US policy will have consequences for the world as a whole.

THE POSTMODERN STATE

The postmodern state defines itself by its security policy. It does so as a matter of political choice. There is no iron law of history that compels states to take the risk of trusting transparency rather than armed force as the best way of preserving its security. Nevertheless only certain kinds of states and societies are likely to make such a choice. Lying behind the postmodern international order is the postmodern state – more pluralist, more complex, less centralized than the bureaucratic modern state, but not at all chaotic, unlike the pre-modern.

As the state itself becomes less dominating, state interest becomes less of a determining factor in foreign policy: the media, popular emotion, the interests of particular groups or regions (including transnational groups) all come into play. The deconstruction of the modern state is not yet complete, but it proceeds rapidly; in their different ways the European

Union, the movement in many countries towards greater regional autonomy, and the more or less universal movement towards privatization, are all part of a process which is creating more pluralistic states in which power is diffused more widely. This development of state structures is matched by a society that is more sceptical of state power, less nationalistic, in which multiple identities thrive and personal development and personal consumption have become the central goals of most people's lives. Army recruitment becomes difficult – consumerism is the one cause for which it makes no sense to die – though fortunately technology means that fewer recruits are required. Where once recruitment posters proclaimed YOUR COUNTRY NEEDS YOU!, they now carry slogans such as JOIN THE ARMY: BE ALL THAT YOU CAN; self-realization has replaced patriotism as a motive for serving in the armed forces. And while soldiers still die bravely for their countries, today they may also sue them for injuries sustained in war.

It is possible to identify (loosely) the three stages of state development with three types of economy: agricultural in the pre-modern; industrial mass production in the modern; and the post-industrial service and information economy with the postmodern state. The postmodern state is one that above all values the individual, which explains its unwarlike character. War is essentially a collective activity: the struggles of the twentieth century have been the struggles of liberalism – the doctrine of the individual – against different forms of collectivism: class, nation, race, community or state. On this basis the United States would also qualify as a postmodern state; and indeed its security policies to its immediate neighbours, Mexico and Canada, as well as towards Europe, are more or less in the postmodern mould. But the United

States is a global power and as such sees its neighbourhood as the world – one that contains too many dangers to rely on trust rather than on its own overwhelming military superiority. Moreover, following their experiences in the twentieth century, most European states have become less nationalist, while America has not. Perhaps this is partly because European nationalism has been associated with ethnicity, whereas American nationalism is defined by loyalty to the constitution, making it easier to preserve in a more diverse society.

All industrial or post-industrial states are potentially postmodern. In the 1930s, however, Germany and the Soviet Union took a different route. In their different ways both fascism and communism were systems designed for war. The ethos and rhetoric of fascism, the uniforms, parades, the glorification of military conflict, all made this plain. As far as fascist governments were concerned the state did not just have a monopoly on violence: violence was its *raison d'être*. Communism also seems, in retrospect, like an attempt to run a state as though it were an army and as if the country were continuously at war. Not for nothing was the term 'command economy' used.

Both communism and fascism were attempts to resist the effects of the modernization of society brought about by the ideas of the Enlightenment and the technology of the Industrial Revolution. This modernization meant that personal ties were replaced by anonymous commercial dealings and instead of the certainties of a life determined by birth and surrounded by family, people found themselves condemned to be free and having to struggle for life and status in a competitive society. Both communism and fascism tried to provide a collectivist refuge for the individual against the loneliness and uncertainty of life in a modernizing society. Both tried to use the state to replace the sense of community that was lost as industrial cities replaced agricultural villages. Both thereby maintained, *inter alia*, the intrusiveness and conformity of the village too: the secret police were the industrial age's equivalent of the village gossip. 'Upper Volta with rockets' (a phrase sometimes used contemptuously to describe the Soviet Union) was in fact exactly what communism aimed at: village life plus state power; technical modernization in a politically primitive setting. Communism and fascism were thus, in this sense, the culmination of the modern, highly centralized state, which sought total control over the lives of its subjects. All the methods that modern states apply in foreign policy (force, spying, secrecy) were used domestically – *raison d'état* made into a system of domestic governance as well as foreign policy.

The postmodern state is the opposite. The individual has won[14] and foreign policy is the continuation of domestic concerns beyond national boundaries and not vice versa. Individual consumption replaces collective glory as the dominant theme of national life. War is to be avoided: acquisition of territory by force is of no interest.

A postmodern order requires postmodern states and vice versa. To create a lasting postmodern security system in Europe it is crucial that all the most powerful European actors should fit into the same pattern. The Cold War could come to an end only through a domestic transformation in the Soviet Union. This is, as yet, neither complete nor certain, but in historical terms progress has been rapid. What has happened, though, probably irreversibly, is a foreign policy transformation.

Russia has largely given up its empire, joining the rest of Europe as a post-imperial state. The last details of this transition remain to be settled – and this could take a long time. Nevertheless, Russia seems to have abandoned its imperialist gains and its imperialist ambitions. This is important for West European countries. No country could feel safe while their neighbour was under enemy occupation or a regime imposed from the outside. In this sense, insecurity is indivisible.

As long as the Soviet Union tried to maintain territorial control over Poland and other Central European states, the possibility of its ambitions stretching further to the West could not be ruled out. Nor need such ambitions be part of a quest for glory or for power: the logic of territorial-based defence is that you always need more territory to defend that which you have acquired. As the Soviet Union lost an empire, the West lost an enemy.

Thus for Western Europe the postmodern age began in 1989. Until then it was all very well for West European states to operate in the postmodern mode within their own circle, but the dominating theme of their foreign and defence policies for the post-war period was the Cold War. That compelled them to base their thinking ultimately on armed protection, secrecy and balance. The hard core of Western policy during this time was that of the modern state. That is now gone. The Europeans are postmodern states living on a postmodern continent.

3
SECURITY IN THE NEW WORLD

Hamlet: What news?
Rosencrantz: None, my lord, but that the world's
                grown honest.
Hamlet: Then is doomsday near.
                        Hamlet (Act II, Scene 2)

This is a new world, but there is neither a new world order (to use a phrase that was fashionable in the early 1990s), nor is there a new world disorder (to use a phrase that has become more fashionable since). Instead there is a zone of safety in Europe and outside it a zone of danger and chaos. What makes this a particularly difficult and dangerous world is that, through globalization, the three zones are interconnected. A world divided into three needs a threefold security policy and a threefold mindset. Neither is easy to achieve.

Before we can think about the security requirements for today and tomorrow, we have to forget the security rules of yesterday. The twentieth century was marked by absolutes. The war against Hitler and the struggle against communism had to be won. The only possible policy was absolute victory, unconditional surrender.

In the more complex and more ambiguous post-war world, we shall not always face the same total threats or need to employ the methods of total war against them. For the most part, therefore, we shall have to discard unconditional surrender as a military or political objective. In none of the three worlds that we live in will complete victory usually be required.

THE WARS OF THE MODERN WORLD

Gulf War I

The most familiar problem for the postmodern state is posed by the modern world of ambitious states. If eventually these states decide to join a postmodern system of open diplomacy, so much the better; but this will take time and between now and then lie many dangers. The first Gulf War provides an illustration both of the dangers and of how they should be dealt with. One ambitious state attacks another, threatening vital Western interests. In the case of Saddam Hussein's invasion of Kuwait, the primary interest was the maintenance of a plurality of states in an area of the world containing vital oil supplies (in global energy terms this is a policy similar to the traditional British requirement that there should be a plurality of powers on the European continent). Had Saddam Hussein been allowed to retain Kuwait, he would have become the geopolitical master of the Gulf. The small Gulf states would have been at his mercy and Saudi Arabia would have been under threat. Preventing this was a sufficient reason for war, but as the campaign developed it became clear that an even greater danger lay in the shape of his programmes of weapons of mass destruction.

The West responded to this classical invasion with a classical counter-invasion. The United States built a powerful coalition, reversed the aggression and punished the aggressor. It set up systems and pressures to disarm Iraq and deal with the weapons programmes. These limited goals required limited means. They did not imply that Iraq should be occupied or that Saddam Hussein should be removed from power (attractive as that idea undoubtedly was). The reference point for a war of this nature is the limited wars of the eighteenth century, not the twentieth-century wars of absolutes. Gulf War I was a war of interests, not a clash of ideologies.

The reason for fighting this war was *not* that Iraq had violated the norms of international behaviour. Unfortunately, the reality is that if one country invades another that lies some way outside the vital interests of the powerful, it will probably get away with it. Very likely it will be condemned and its territorial gains will not be recognized. It will lose trust and reputation. It might suffer economic sanctions for a while. But the invader will probably not be attacked by the powerful. If India were to invade Nepal, for example, or Argentina Paraguay, it is unlikely that a Gulf War-style coalition would be put together to reverse the result.

The initial enthusiasm for the idea of a new world order[15] that followed Gulf War I was based on the hope that the United Nations was going to function as originally intended: a world authority policing international law, that is to say a collective-security organization. That hope was not entirely unreasonable. The end of the Cold War took the world back to 1945. While institutions that had grown up because of – or against the background of – the Cold War, such as NATO or the European Union, began to look in need of radical change, the United Nations was a pre-Cold War institution and, therefore, might become a workable post-Cold War institution. Up to a point this proved to be the case. The United Nations is more active today than it ever was during the Cold War (between 1946 and 1990 there were 683 Security Council Resolutions; in the thirteen years since then the number has more than doubled; and as many as 500,000 UN troops have been deployed at certain times).

The United Nations however, is more active in peace-keeping and humanitarian work than as a collective-security organization. And the new world order, which at one time attracted such hope, was that of a collective-security order.

A collective-security order is one in which the international community enforces international law on recalcitrant states. This was the idea behind both the League of Nations and the United Nations: collective action against violators of international law. This would certainly be a new order in the sense that we have never seen such a system function in practice, from the Abyssinian crisis to the present day. Unfortunately, we are never likely to see it either.

Some mistook Gulf War I for a war of principles or a collective-security action – and indeed the political rhetoric at the time fostered this impression. In fact, it was a collective defence of interests by the West. As a number of people remarked at the time: if Kuwait had produced carrots rather than oil, it is most unlikely that a great coalition would have assembled to reverse Iraqi aggression. Gulf War I was fought to protect the old order, not to create a new one.

In a different sense, though, a collective-security order would not really be new. Collective-security is a combination of two older ideas: stability through balance and stability through hegemony. The *status quo* is maintained by a world body of overwhelming power (the hegemonic element), which throws its weight on the side of a state that is the victim of aggression – the balance of power, that is, with the world community as the balancing actor.

This is the old world of state sovereignty in which others do not interfere, of coalitions, of security through military force. The United Nations, as a collective-security organization, is there to defend the *status quo* and not to create a new order. And, indeed, the new postmodern European order described above is based on entirely different ideas.

The wars in the former Yugoslavia
The story of the wars in the former Yugoslavia and of the Western intervention there is a more complicated one. The former Yugoslavia contains elements of the post-imperial/pre-modern world where weak states barely have control over the means of force. For the longer term many of the states there clearly have some postmodern aspirations. But the dominant feature so far has been the creation of the modern nation states of Croatia and Serbia.[16]

Western intervention has been above all in support of the individual – humanitarian intervention began out of good postmodern motives. But it ran into the ambitions of Milosevic's thoroughly modern nationalistic state. The first major clash, over Bosnia, was eventually handled more or less according to the recipe outlined above for Gulf War I – a mixture of limited force and negotiation – with a certain measure of success. The second episode, in Kosovo, was rather different. Here the humanitarian mission concerned the situation within Serbia. The military campaign was fought – as it turned out entirely with air power – to enforce certain minimum values on a state unwilling to respect them. Unlike Gulf War I this was an action fought for principle and, unlike the general rule in postmodern Europe, it involved intervention in the domestic affairs of the state, not by mutual consent but by force. The basis of this action has been described by Tony Blair in what might be taken as a classic statement of postmodern aspirations:

We have to enter the new millennium making it known to dictatorships that ethnic cleansing will not be approved. And if we fight, it is not for territorial imperatives but for values. For a new internationalism where the brutal repression of ethnic groups will not be tolerated. For a world where those responsible for crimes will have nowhere to hide.[17]

It is worth quoting at length the most forceful criticism of this approach. Henry Kissinger writes:

The abrupt abandonment of the concept of national sovereignty... marked the advent of a new style of foreign policy driven by domestic politics and the invocation of universal moralistic slogans... Those who sneer at history obviously do not recall that the legal doctrine of national sovereignty and the principle of non-interference – enshrined in the UN Charter – emerged at the end of the devastating Thirty Years War.

The new discipline of international law sought to inhibit repetition of the depredations of the religious wars of the seventeenth century during which perhaps 40 per cent of the population of Central Europe perished in the name of competing versions of universal truth. Once the doctrine of universal intervention spreads and competing truths contest we risk entering a world in which, in G. K. Chesterton's phrase, 'virtue runs amok'.[18]

In answer to this, supporters of postmodern intervention would probably argue that they were not, for the moment at least, contemplating universal intervention. But there is a second, more important point. Europe, perhaps for the first time in 300 years, is no longer a zone of competing truths. The end of the Cold War has brought with it something like a common set of values in Europe. It is this that makes postmodern intervention sustainable, both morally and practically, in the European context. One of the most striking features of the Kosovo intervention was its unanimous support across a group of NATO governments representing every point on the political spectrum. Against the background of the wars in the Balkans and the crimes associated with them there was something close to a consensus for action. Perhaps equally important was the collective memory of the Holocaust and the streams of displaced people created by extreme nationalism in the Second World War. Common European values have grown out of this common historical experience, which, in extreme cases, can provide a justification for armed intervention. It would be a very different thing to intervene in another continent with another history and would require a rather greater risk of humanitarian catastrophe. The European order is based on a specific European history and the values that flow from it. A universal order is still limited by the relatively narrow consensus on universal values.

This does not mean that intervention for values will be easy. It is dangerous to become involved in wars of principle; it is difficult to call them off if they go wrong and equally difficult to sustain them if casualties mount. And besides, war is essentially destructive. One can punish those who transgress principles, but it is difficult to use force to implement them. Bombs can flatten cities, but they cannot create the rule of law or non-discrimination in employment; troops can keep order, but they cannot create a sense of community or a culture of tolerance.

For the postmodern state there is, therefore, a difficulty. It needs to get used to the idea of double standards. Among themselves, the postmodern states operate on the basis of laws and open co-operative security. But when dealing with more old-fashioned kinds of state outside the postmodern limits, Europeans need to revert to the rougher methods of an earlier era – force, pre-emptive attack, deception, whatever is necessary for those who still live in the nineteenth-century world of every state for itself.

In the jungle, one must use the laws of the jungle. In this period of peace in Europe, there is a temptation to neglect defences, both physical and psychological. This represents one of the dangers for the postmodern state.

Gulf War II: weapons of mass destruction
There is, however, a second set of forces at work that reinforces the position of the modern state and could radically change the structures of international relations. These arise from the potential spread of Weapons of Mass Destruction – the origin, in part at least – of Gulf War II. For fifty years the spread of nuclear weapons has been contained, partly because most countries decided they did not want them, partly through controls on the materials and technology necessary to make them. In the 1990s the world received two shocks. India and Pakistan reminded the international community that they both had nuclear weapons; and then demonstrated in a series of crises that their use could not be altogether excluded. Second, and even more alarming, was the discovery during Gulf War I that Iraq was within a few months of having a workable nuclear device and also had extensive chemical and biological programmes. This suggested that the time bought by policies designed to contain proliferation was running out and that the West might soon have to face the possibility of further countries acquiring nuclear or other weapons capable of causing unacceptable loss of life.

If this were to happen we would be living in a radically different world. The Cold War eventually achieved nuclear stability and, through an understanding of the risks that instability might bring, this was extended to encompass conventional stability too. But the Cold War was a bipolar system managed by two rather cautious countries sharing at least some historical and cultural common ground. Even so, there were several uncomfortable moments on the way to stability. The more countries acquire nuclear weapons the more other countries will want them too. At a certain point, those who have accepted self-imposed restraints would be compelled to review their position. An international system in which several countries held nuclear weapons would no longer function along classical balance-of-power principles. In fact we do not know how it would function. In such a world the search for a new international equilibrium by the usual processes of trial and error would have devastating consequences. For the first time the international legal ideal of a world of sovereign equality would be fulfilled – since with nuclear weapons (provided you have a second-strike capability) all countries are equal and a nuclear armed minnow can still inflict unacceptable damage on a great power.

All that is certain is that the more countries that have nuclear weapons the more will want them; and the more that get them the more unstable the system will become and the greater the risk that sooner or later (probably sooner) someone will use them. Proliferation is a threat not just to this or that individual country, but to the whole system of interstate relations. It seems likely that it would lead not so much to instability as to nuclear armed anarchy; a world of independent states, each capable of destroying the other, and some capable of destroying the world.

This is the nightmare of the modern. Preventing it should be a priority for all who wish to live in a reasonably orderly world. The question is how this can be done. Following well-established legal norms and relying on self-defence will not solve the problem. Not only is self-defence too late after a nuclear attack, but it misses a wider point. Nuclear war affects those who are not directly involved: through fall-out and contamination. A nuclear exchange would give a further spur to proliferation and would remove the taboo on further use of nuclear weapons. Since the more countries that have nuclear weapons the more likely use becomes, the only rational policy is to stop the spread in the first place. This is a vital interest for the whole civilized world. It would be irresponsible to do nothing while even one further country acquires nuclear capability. Nor is it good enough to wait until that country acquires the bomb. By then the costs of military action may be too high. Hence the doctrine of preventative action in the US National Security Strategy. In practice this is not so different from the longstanding British doctrine that no single power should be allowed to dominate the continent of Europe. This gave rise, for example, to the War of the Spanish Succession, fought to ensure that the crowns of France and Spain were not united. This also was a preventative war. No one attacked Britain; but if Britain had allowed the two countries to unite it would by then have been unable to deal with an attack from the resulting super-power. Nuclear weapons make every country potentially too strong to deal with.

If everyone adopted a preventative doctrine the world could degenerate into chaos, not perhaps as bad as nuclear anarchy, but highly unstable as countries tried to second-guess their neighbours and get their retaliation in first. (The doctrine of preventative war was one of the factors leading up to the start of the First World War). A system in which preventative action is required will be stable only under the condition that it is dominated by a single power or a concert of powers. The doctrine of prevention therefore needs to be complemented by a doctrine of enduring strategic superiority – and this is, in fact, the main theme of the US National Security Strategy.

If the spread of nuclear weapons becomes the major theme in international relations then we might find that the world tends towards an order dominated by a single hegemonic power. Whether such a system lasts will depend on whether it is seen as legitimate by a sufficient number of other actors. In practice, a coalition or concert will be necessary, since for America to fill this role alone would involve too high a cost at home and too much resentment abroad. But this will be a different and more difficult world from the one we have grown used to. Nuclear weapons are an absolute, just as the ideologies of the twentieth century were. Neither permits compromise. Rational argument and negotiated solutions may be defeated by the consuming imperative of security.

SECURITY AND THE PRE-MODERN WORLD

What of the pre-modern chaos? What should be done with that? At the start of the 1990s it seemed that the answer was: as little as possible. Chaos does not represent a threat of the kind we are used to – an armed attack by the military of an aggressive neighbouring state. The chaos in Somalia and the breakdown of the state in parts of the former Yugoslavia excited pity, anger and shame, but they did not represent a direct threat to the lives or livelihoods of those living in safer, better organized territories. True, the region of chaos might give rise to unattractive by-products – drugs, disease, refugees – but these are not the sort of threats to vital interests that normally call for armed Western intervention. To become involved in a zone of chaos is expensive and risky; if the intervention is prolonged it may become unsustainable in public opinion; if it is unsuccessful it may be damaging to the government that ordered it. Thus the initial Western response to the situation in the Balkans, in Somalia or Afghanistan was a combination of neglect, half-hearted peace efforts, plus a humanitarian attempt to deal with the symptoms, while steering clear of the (possibly infectious) disease.

Since then Western governments have learned three things about the pre-modern state and the chaos it represents, all of them dangerous. And it may be that there are more lessons to come: our knowledge of this phenomenon is still shallow. First, they have learned that chaos spreads. Sierra Leone's collapse into anarchy helped destabilize Liberia; the growing lawlessness in Liberia has in turn endangered its neighbours – including Sierra Leone itself, just as it seemed to be on the road to recovery. In Central Africa the chaos of the DRC (the former Belgian Congo) is linked to the tragic events in Rwanda and the fragility of Burundi. Around Afghanistan there have been risks to Pakistan and to the Central Asian republics, Tajikistan and Uzbekistan. When a state ceases to function, its borders cease to function too.

Part of the reason for this – and this is the second lesson – is that when states collapse crime takes over. This is, in a sense, logical. When it functions properly the state exercises both a monopoly on force and a monopoly on law. As it loses its monopoly on force, the law also ceases to exist and is replaced by privatized violence and private profit as the principles governing the territory. Pre-modern states are usually the scene of a series of conflicts – initially civil wars, later the wars of all against all (as Hobbes so aptly named them) – for the control of resources. These may be minerals (the ruthenium mines in Sierra Leone or gold in Rwanda); they may be precious stones, as in Central Africa and parts of Afghanistan; they may be drugs or trade in people – refugees or sex-slaves. Gemstones (now often called 'conflict diamonds' or 'blood diamonds') are especially convenient since they are easily carried, concealed and marketed – though the international community is now attempting to put an end to this trade by means of a system of certificates of origin. And although the state has ceased to be a real power, capturing the institutions of the state can still be lucrative. It offers opportunities for obtaining aid funds, bribes and a certain prestige. Even in conditions of chaos it is still the ultimate prize.

This descent into criminality matters to the developed world of modern and postmodern states because crime also spreads. Pre-modern states are too poor to provide good revenue for the criminal gangs taking over a state or fighting for control of parts of its territory. Diamonds, drugs and the unlucky girls who are sold into prostitution have to be marketed abroad. Arms have to be purchased. Criminal interests may be based in the pre-modern, but they will have branch offices in the West. At a certain point these groups could become powerful enough to threaten Western security as well as that of their victims in the pre-modern world. Not in every case – the nearer are more dangerous than the distant – but the option of tackling the problem at source should be kept in mind.

This brings the third lesson, which was learned on 11 September 2001. Sometimes a zone of chaos can turn into a major direct threat to state security elsewhere. It is true that the circumstances of Afghanistan were unique. What was left of the state was dominated by an extreme Islamist regime that contracted out different state functions to different bodies: finance to drug barons, health and welfare to the United Nations and various NGOs, and defence to Osama bin Laden. In return for shelter and facilities to train terrorists he provided men and arms to prosecute the civil war against Ahmed Masood. (Possibly he also helped to organize the assassination of Masood. It seems too much of a coincidence that this took place only days before the attack on America.) The fighters and the terrorists came from a variety of sources; some of the 'Arab Legion' had fought in the Balkans, some in Chechnya; some were from Pakistan; a few were from the West. All, terrorists and fighters, were Muslims, many of them participants in some way in the crisis that has affected the Islamic world in the Middle East and North Africa over several decades. It is unlikely that these specific circumstances will ever arise again – or that the West will allow them to. (That Western governments knew of terrorist training camps and allowed them to continue in operation is, in retrospect, extraordinary.) But the lesson remains that chaos in critical parts of the world should not unwatched go. It was not the well-organized Persian Empire that brought about the fall of Rome, but the barbarians.

The difficulty, however, is in knowing what form intervention should take: the most logical way to deal with chaos is by colonization. If the nation state has failed why not go back to an older form – empire? The nation state has been a powerful engine of progress but it is far from having been a total success. In its European birthplace it led to an interstate system where, in the end, balance broke down and the states themselves exceeded all the bounds of the restraint necessary to make the system function. Strangely, just as European countries, after two devastating wars, were adopting a framework that reduced the exclusiveness of the nation state and the clarity of its division from its neighbours, they were bequeathing the nation state system in its original form to their imperial subjects abroad. The very act of decolonization was itself a last imperial imposition since it gave to Africans and Asians a system based on a purely European model and alien to their own history. Nor has the nation state functioned brilliantly outside Europe. Its first exponent in the Far East, Japan, demonstrated such dynamism compared with its neighbours that it devastated the whole region and ended by devastating itself. Since then Japan and other countries have survived more comfortably under a benign American hegemony. In Africa and the Middle East the nation state has been a manifest failure both for individual countries, their citizens, and for the region as a whole.

However, there can be no return to imperialism in its traditional form. Empire does not work in a post-imperial age. No Western country believes enough in their civilizing mission to impose their own rule permanently by force; nor could this be done, since the Western ideology is democratic and democracy cannot be achieved by coercion (though armies can create the conditions for it by removing dictators). Nor would traditional imperialism be acceptable to the peoples of failed states – except perhaps in an initial phase when they are rescued from chaos or tyrants. The imperial experience is still fresh in the memories of its victims and it was not, on the whole, a pleasant one.

Nation state and empire are in some respects opposites: empires are diverse; nation states are uniform. National states are limited by the geography of language. Empires in the older tradition – such as the Roman or the Ottoman Empire – had no difficulty in expanding: all newly acquired people could become citizens, in theory at least. An empire created by a national state was different. The state was founded on a cultural or even a racial identity and could not absorb foreigners easily. That left only two alternatives: the option of consigning the conquered people to an inferior status in a racist empire – which is the route taken by the nineteenth-century European nation states; or the option of annihilating the conquered or making them slaves, the logical conclusion of extreme nationalism in the twentieth century. The nation state may be liberal, but liberal imperialism is a contradiction in terms. Nineteenth-century empires were based on shared racist assumptions – both colonizers and colonized seemed to have accepted the idea of white superiority. But these assumptions are gone. The postmodern version of empire has to be voluntary if it is to be acceptable; if it is to last it has to be co-operative.

A limited form of voluntary empire is provided by the programmes of assistance of the IMF and the World Bank. In return for financial support, which offers a way back into the global economy, a country accepts advice and supervision. This may sometimes take the form of foreign officials sitting in ministries giving advice – which is not in the end very different from giving orders. In 1875 the developed world dealt with the Egyptian financial crisis in a rather similar way: a British committee representing bond-holders supervised the revenues of the Egyptian government, while a French committee supervised expenditures. The similarity with the case of an IMF programme ended, however, when the Egyptian government was overthrown (as sometimes happens with IMF programmes too) and the new one threatened to ignore the programme. Instead of trying to renegotiate – as the IMF would today – Britain sent General Wolseley, with 31,000 men, to restore order and good government.

A financial crisis may be dealt with by a limited form of (voluntary) imperialism confined to the financial sector. When a crisis is more general – and the international community cares sufficiently – a more far-reaching form is required. This general imperialism, also voluntary, takes the form of trusteeship, usually exercised by the international community through the United Nations, as in Bosnia, Kosovo and Afghanistan. It was exercised temporarily in East Timor and even more briefly in Cambodia. It gives the people of a failed state a breathing space and some international assistance to enable them to re-establish a more sustainable state. These arrangements are not as efficient as traditional imperialism. Because it is voluntary, everything is subject to negotiation and compromise; because the administering authority is international, it lacks the clarity, decisiveness and accountability of a national power; because it is temporary, the chances are it will leave before the job is done properly. Nevertheless, in a postmodern era, international and voluntary spells legitimate and in the end nothing else will work.

The most far-reaching form of imperial expansion is that of the European Union. In the last few years countries all across central Europe have transformed their constitutions, rewritten their laws, adjusted the rules of their markets, set up anti-corruption bodies and adopted a huge volume of EU legislation – all in the interests of becoming members of the Union. The changes in Turkey, where the death penalty has been abolished and minority rights established, are especially striking. In another age, such changes would have taken place only in the context of a takeover by a colonial power, but today's reforms have been undertaken voluntarily with a view to joining the empire, securing a seat at its table and a voice in its government. This form of empire is likely to last, since its co-operative structure gives it a lasting legitimacy; 'commonwealth' would be a better name for it. The lure of membership plays a vital part in stabilizing the Balkans and in encouraging reform elsewhere on the margins of the European Union. The impossibility of subdividing countries into ever smaller ethnic units (one of the reasons why the national state functions poorly in an age that values self-determination) suggests that, in areas of ethnic diversity, a wider governance, similar to that of older empires, might have more chance of success than the national state.

Left alone, few of the new member states of the European Union would have become failed states, but it does them no harm to be able to take constitutional models and systems of regulation off the shelf; and there are advantages in belonging to a body that can help defend their interests in dealings with continental-sized countries like the United States and, in the future, China. For others, however, the European Union may offer a solution to problems that the nation state was unable to solve. Cyprus, for example, survived reasonably well as a part of the Venetian, Ottoman and British Empires. As a nation state it has not worked. But perhaps, in the postmodern European empire, it might one day be able to return to a normal existence.

Empire is expensive, especially in its postmodern voluntary form. Nation-building is a long and difficult task: it is by no means certain that any of the recent attempts are going to be successful. Great caution is required for anyone contemplating intervention in the pre-modern chaos. A good rule would be to intervene early before the trouble really begins. But this is not easy either. No state will readily accept that radical interference from outside is needed to prevent its collapse; nor will outsiders want to take on the risks and costs of intervention until it is proved to them that there is no other solution (by which time it is usually too late).

Humanitarian interventions are particularly dangerous for those who intervene. It is difficult to set clear objectives: it is difficult to know where to stop. The risk of 'mission creep' is considerable. Those who become involved in the pre-modern world run the risk that ultimately they will be there because they are there. Intervention motivated by power and interest are more likely to be sustainable and are therefore more likely to be successful. All the conventional wisdom and all realistic doctrines of international affairs counsel against military involvement in the pre-modern world out of purely altruistic motives.

And yet, for all their intellectual coherence, these 'realistic' doctrines are not realistic. Although some lessons have been learned in Somalia and Bosnia, there will always be new cases and new disasters. The post-Cold War, postmodern environment is one in which foreign policy will be driven partly by domestic politics; and these will be influenced by the media and by moral sentiment. We no longer live in a world of purely national interest. Human rights and humanitarian problems inevitably play a part in our policy-making.

A new world order might not be a reality, but it is an important aspiration, especially for those living in a new European order. The wish to protect individuals, rather than to resolve the security problems of states, is part of the postmodern ethos. In a world where many states suffer breakdowns there is wide scope for humanitarian intervention. Operations in these areas are a halfway house between the calculation of interest, which tells you not to get involved, and the moral feeling of the public that 'something must be done'. In different ways, all these operations have been directed towards helping civilians – against the military, the government or the chaos. The results are not always impressive and the interventions are in some respects half-hearted. This is because they inhabit an ambiguous half-world where interest tells you to stay out and conscience tells you to go in – between Hobbes and Kant.

Such interventions may not solve problems, but they may salve the conscience; and they may save some lives in the process. They are not necessarily the worse for that.

Thus we must reconcile ourselves to the fact that we are going to get involved in situations where interest and calculation would tell us to stay out. In this case, there are some rules to observe. The first is to moderate the objectives to the means available. The wars of ideology called for total victory; the wars of interests call for victory; in the pre-modern world victory is not a relevant objective.

Victory in the pre-modern world would mean empire and neither side might be ready for that. The postmodern power that has intervened to save the lives of individual civilians usually wants to stop short of empire. In consequence, goals must be even more carefully defined than in wars of interest. They should be expressed in relatives rather than absolutes: more lives saved, lower levels of violence among the local populations; and these goals must be balanced by low casualties for those who intervene. At the same time, Western governments must be prepared to accept – indeed must expect – failure some of the time. And then they must be prepared to cut their losses and leave. The operation in Somalia was not a success for anybody. And yet it was not unreasonable to try (though the trial might have been better organized). And it was not unreasonable to get out when it did not work. The attempt gave those responsible in Somalia a breathing space, a chance to sort themselves out. That they failed to take that chance was not the fault of the intervention force.

It follows also that when intervening in the pre-modern world, Clausewitz's doctrine still applies: war is the pursuit of politics by other means. Military intervention should always be accompanied by political efforts. If these fail, or if the cost of the military operation becomes too great, then there is no alternative but to withdraw.

CONCLUSION: SECURITY AND THE POSTMODERN WORLD

That there is no new world order is a common conception. It is less widely understood that there is a new European order: new in that it is historically unprecedented and also because it is based on new concepts. Indeed, the order preceded the concepts. One commentator who fails to understand this – though he understands most things better than the rest of us and describes them with great elegance and clarity – is Henry Kissinger: 'In a world of players of operationally more or less equal strength, there are only two roads to stability. One is hegemony and the other is equilibrium.'[19] This was the choice in the past, but today it no longer works. Balance is unstable and that is now too dangerous. Hegemony breeds resentment. It is difficult to accept in a liberal world that values human rights and self-determination.

Instead, there is a third possibility: postmodern security. In fact, there have been three sets of alternatives: first came the choice between chaos and empire; anarchy or a central monopoly on power. Then it was a choice between empire and nationalism: centralized authority or a balance of power. Today, finally, we have a choice between nationalism and integration: balance or openness. Chaos is tamed by empire; empires are broken up by nationalism; nationalism gives way, we must hope, to internationalism. At the end of the process is the freedom of the individual; first protected by the state and later protected from the state.

The kind of world we have depends on the kind of states that compose it: for the pre-modern world, success is empire and failure is chaos. For the modern, success entails managing the balance of power and failure means falling back into war or empire. For the postmodern state, success means openness and transnational co-operation. (Failure we shall come to in a moment.) The open state system is the ultimate consequence of the open society.

This categorization is not intended to be exclusive – the future is full of surprises (and so, indeed, is the past). Nor is it intended to represent some inevitable Hegelian progression. Progress it certainly represents, but there is nothing inevitable about it. In particular, there is nothing inevitable about the survival of the postmodern state in what remains a difficult environment.

The postmodern European order faces the same dangers as the United States. First, there is the danger from the pre-modern. We may not be interested in chaos but chaos is interested in us. In fact chaos, or at least the crime that lives within it, needs the civilized world and preys upon it. Open societies make this easy. At its worst, in the form of terrorism, chaos can become a serious threat to the whole international order. Terrorism represents the privatization of war, the pre-modern with teeth; if terrorists use biological or nuclear weapons the effects could be devastating. This is the non-state attacking the state. A lesser danger is the risk of being sucked into the pre-modern for reasons of conscience and then being unwilling either to take over or to get out. In the end, this process would be debilitating for morale and dangerous for military preparedness.

The second major danger is from the modern. There is no state that is likely to want to invade Europe either today or for the foreseeable future. In a more distant future an armed and ambitious China or India could upset the regional balance and threaten European interests, but a direct attack on the European continent seems improbable. The real threat from the modern is likely to come in the form of weapons of mass destruction, a danger which again Europe shares with the United States.

The two approaches to dealing with these threats have been described earlier in this essay. The US approach is based on hegemony: control – by military means if necessary – of the foreign policies of all potentially threatening states. The weakness of this approach is that the task may be too great even for the United States. Power may be distributed too widely for easy control; if too many interventions are required, the costs of sustaining them may become too high. At the same time intervention creates resentment and fear: the cure may spread the disease rather than end it.

The postmodern, European answer to threats is to extend the system of co-operative empire ever wider. 'I have no way to defend my borders but to extend them,' said Catherine the Great – and the European Union sometimes seems to be saying the same. This is, in fact, an exact description of the most natural security policy for a postmodern community of states. The wider the postmodern network can be extended, the less risk there will be from neighbours and the more resources to defend the community without having to become excessively militarized. (The Roman Empire in its later stages had similar advantages, though it threw them away by neglecting its defences altogether.) Although the European Union grew up under the wing of US military power this is not essential for its long-term survival, provided it can achieve a critical mass – which it has already done – and provided it can achieve a robust defence culture – where it has still some way to go. Even so, this policy has limitations. First, it relies on the spread of European political culture. For many of Europe's neighbours this amounts to regime change – and even where this is possible it is likely to be a slow business. Second, there are obvious geographical constraints; the European commonwealth has to be more or less contiguous, but the threats, in a globalized world, can come from anywhere.

Though different, these approaches are not incompatible with each other. It may be that some combination of the two policies can be made to work: military muscle to clear the way for a political solution involving a kind of imperial penumbra around the European Union might be an attractive way to deal with the area of greatest threat in the Middle East. If Europe is serious, however, it needs to contribute more in the field of military muscle. The future is determined not just by grand designs and treaties, but by the decisions that are taken on the ground by force commanders in Afghanistan and Iraq. Co-operative empire is an attractive dream, but until it comes true – and it may never happen – the postmodern space needs to be able to protect itself. States reared on *raison d'état* and power politics make uncomfortable neighbours for the postmodern democratic conscience. Supposing the world develops (as Kissinger suggests it might) into an intercontinental struggle. Would Europe be equipped for that?

The third danger is specific to the postmodern European world and comes from within. A postmodern world in which security interests are not uppermost in people's minds is one where the state becomes less important. Within the shelter of NATO and the European Union the state itself may weaken or fragment – if devolution turns to disintegration. A medieval patchwork of states may be too diverse to organize and too diffuse to allow the decisiveness required in security matters. Historically, the state has been by far the most efficient actor in the security field. The next decades will show whether a union of states can be as effective in dealing with external threats as it has been in eliminating internal conflicts.

A postmodern economy can have the result that everyone lives only for themselves and not at all for the community – the decline of birth rates in the West is already evidence of this tendency. There is a risk, too, that the deconstruction of the state may spill over into the deconstruction of society. In political terms, an excess of transparency and an over-diffusion of power could lead to a state, and to an international order, in which nothing can be done and nobody is accountable because there is no central focus of power or responsibility. We may all drown in complexity.

It may be that in Western Europe the era of the strong state – 1648 to 1989 – has now passed and we are moving towards a system of overlapping roles and responsibilities with governments, international institutions and the private sector all involved, but none of them entirely in control. Can it be made to work? We must hope so and we must try.

PART TWO
THE CONDITIONS OF PEACE:
TWENTY-FIRST CENTURY
DIPLOMACY

INTRODUCTION

'Words alone are certain good.'
W. B. Yeats, 'The Song of the Happy Shepherd'

This is a dangerous world and it is going to become more dangerous. The twin dangers of terrorism and weapons of mass destruction present us with a radically altered security environment. Conflict will bring greater loss than ever before. It is essential that we start now on the search for political solutions to our problems and those of others. In the past it was enough for a nation to look after itself. Today that is no longer sufficient. In an age of globalization no country is an island. Crises in Kashmir, the Middle East or the Korean Peninsula affect security in every continent and are the concern of everybody.

The old solutions to the problems of international order – balance or hegemony – do not appear attractive. If balance is going to mean balance among a growing number of states armed with nuclear weapons or other WMD, then it is more likely to be a problem than a solution. In the past the balance of power relied on occasional wars to rebalance the system or to deter aggressors. In a nuclear age that is no longer acceptable.

The alternative of hegemony is not necessarily better. One way to ensure that such weapons do not proliferate might be to establish a benign hegemony of the United States. But that would also raise many problems and would solve few. The task is probably too big for a single country. And however benign it might be, the hegemony would cause resentment and fear. Out of this would come further terrorism and perhaps further proliferation of WMD. Even a wider hegemony including Europe and Japan, while softer at the edges, would not seem very different to those on the receiving end of its attentions.

If neither balance nor hegemony is going to provide security then another solution must be found. Part I of this book described the alternative that has developed in postwar Europe: a community of post-national, post-imperial states living together in historically unprecedented stability and security. Something like this, if it could ever be achieved, will be needed on an international scale – the beginning of a real international society. This essay explores the difficulties in achieving this.

Soldiers and diplomats are, in the end, trying to do the same thing: to change other people's minds. And both are subject to the same problems: not knowing what is in those minds nor how they will react when you try to change them.

Mistakes in foreign policy can be as disastrous as mistakes in war. Sometimes it is hard to distinguish between the two. Britain's loss of its American colonies in the eighteenth century was first and foremost a political failure that eventually manifested itself in military terms. Was the Vietnam War a military or a foreign policy failure? Probably both, but the political failure came first. Conversely, President Kennedy's handling of the Cuban missile crisis was a diplomatic triumph; but it was also a military triumph, because force was an integral part of his strategy. The massacre of Bosnians by Serb militias at Srebrenica was both a diplomatic and a military failure; and the negotiations at Dayton that ended the war in Bosnia were a success for diplomacy, but also for armed force. When diplomacy is not about avoiding war it is about choosing to fight the right war at the right time with the right allies. It is every bit as serious as war itself.

But whereas professional soldiers try, almost as a matter of routine, to learn from the past, there is little equivalent effort in the diplomatic world. Military history is studied by all serious soldiers, but diplomatic history seems to be written by scholars for scholars.

This essay is an attempt to set out some maxims for diplomacy. They are neither rules nor principles; rather they are matter upon which to reflect. The world is fluid. Context, mood and personality all play a greater role in international relations than the textbooks might suggest. Diplomacy is an art not a science. Great creative statesmen can make up the rules as they go along and sometimes do so brilliantly. But for others there is much to be said for trying to learn from experience.

The starting point is what might be described as a postmodern perspective. The objective of foreign policy is taken to be peace and prosperity rather than power and prestige. Power is vital for the defence of peace, but it is a means rather than an end in itself. Thus these are maxims for a post-imperial age and for post-imperial powers. In pre-modern[20] times war was a way of life; in the modern era it was an instrument of policy; but in the postmodern world war has become something to be avoided if at all possible. The use of force is a failure of policy rather than an instrument of policy. We have come from Hobbes and the war of all against all, through Clausewitz, for whom war was the continuation of policy, and have finally returned to Sun Tzu, the Chinese Taoist military philosopher, who argued that the best war was one that did not have to be fought.

Samuel Huntington has written that future wars may be

about who you are rather than what you do or whose side you are on. That, in a sense, is also a theme of this essay. Future peace will also be about who you are. The world is still divided into Them and Us, but (and here, perhaps, I differ from Huntington) sometimes there are opportunities for Us to decide how we define ourselves and, by the same token, how we define others.

Although this essay is written as a commentary on five maxims, it is intended to form a single argument. It may be helpful to the reader to begin with an overview of the argument.

- The first maxim concerns the need to understand foreigners better. This (rather obvious, but much neglected) thought has never been more relevant. Until the end of the Cold War the central preoccupation of Western policy has been with countries and people from similar cultural traditions. In the West, wars were fought by Christians against Christians. Even communism was a bastard child of the Enlightenment and of Christian culture. The problems of the new era will come from cultures that are little understood in the West. The effort required to understand them and the risks of not doing so are alarmingly great.
- The second maxim concerns the fact that even in an age of globalization people's lives and their countries' politics remain stubbornly local. This is also true of foreign policy. 'Think global and act local' may be a good slogan for business, but it leaves diplomats helpless since foreigners are by definition outsiders with little scope to act in the local arena. For a foreign policy to make an impact it has, somehow, to get under the domestic skin.

- This leads to the consideration in the third maxim of the difficulty of influencing foreign governments. One may bribe them, but they stop listening when the money runs out; one may threaten them, even defeat them militarily and occupy their territory, but they can change their policy when the army goes home; or one may try to persuade them. In the end what matters is probably the willingness to make long-term commitments. The best way to use force may well be in a policy of containment: defending one's own country while seeking ways to change others.
- The difficulty in this, as the fourth maxim argues, is that the fundamentals of a country's policy go deeper than its national interests. Negotiating about interests is useful, but the real question is how those interests are defined. This is probably connected to the identity of the country and its people. Securing lasting change is therefore something that goes beyond a negotiation over interests.
- Therefore, to find permanent solutions we may need to think in terms of redefining identity. Only if a wider identity can be developed will there be a chance of constructing the kind of international community that may enable us to live with each other without war.

Viewing the world only as a struggle for power and interest may lead to the illusion that change can be obtained through power and the use of force. Occasionally it can. And force remains vital to establish order and to defend freedom. But more often force is an ineffective way of changing people's minds. Sometimes to change their ways of thinking we need to be ready to change our own as well. Internationally, lasting solutions are about finding a common legitimacy. That might even involve changing our ideas about what we mean by 'foreign'.

Ultimately there are two sources of power: force and legitimacy. People obey out of fear of violence or out of respect for authority. Civilization and order come from putting force at the service of legitimate authority. The instruments of force and ideas of legitimacy change with time and technology. But both force and legitimacy remain essential to order. Force without legitimacy brings chaos; legitimacy without force will be overthrown.

Maxim 1
Foreigners are different

Foreign policy would be easy if it weren't for the foreigners.

Lord Macartney's embassy to the Chinese Emperor in 1793 – an expedition of several hundred men, which spent many months in China – was intended to establish relations between the British and Chinese Empires and, in particular, to open the possibility of trade. The Emperor and the court ignored Macartney's trade requests altogether. The Chinese interpreted the visit as one from an outlying land that wished to place itself under the benevolent rule of the Chinese Emperor. They recorded Macartney as saying: 'It is with the greatest humility that our king sent us to bring his tribute to the Great Emperor.' They generously forgave him for insolently requesting to trade with the empire: 'Having been unaware of the usages of the Empire you presented indecent requests... you shall inform your sovereign that the Great Emperor agrees not to hold him responsible for the errors he has committed with regard to the celestial institutions, of which he was ignorant.' Perhaps there was no other way for the Chinese to interpret the visit. On his side, Macartney – who had refused to perform all of the correct kowtows – reported that he had been received as the ambassador of a sovereign state and that the Emperor had heard, but not replied to his requests. For him too, perhaps, there was no other way in which he could have interpreted his visit. As Alain Peyrefitte records in *The Collision of Two Civilisations* (1989), the process of mutual misunderstanding continued – the element of wilful misunderstanding growing ever more significant – until, in 1839, diplomatic dialogue was abandoned and instead the guns spoke in the Opium Wars.

It is hardly surprising that two such different and distant civilizations as Georgian Britain and Qing China should misunderstand each other. Since then it has become a little easier; but the Chinese vocabulary of sincerity and of the carefully graded apology remains very different from the Western diplomatic tradition. Even if China pursues its interests in much the same way as Western countries, it does so in a language that is easy for others to misread.

The most common method of misunderstanding foreigners is to assume that they are similar to you – which is what both Macartney and the Chinese court did. Khrushchev, 170 years later, made the same mistake when he interpreted Kennedy's use of a back-channel for communication with him as a sign of weakness. The back-channel was in fact a part of the rather personalized, free-wheeling style of the Kennedy team (it was Bobby who operated it). Khrushchev's view was that someone would resort to this kind of secrecy only if they needed to get around a hostile governmental machine: something which would probably have been true if the back-channel had been invented by the Russian leader.

It is easy to multiply examples, serious and trivial. One example of a more trivial sort is the trip made by a leading figure in the Salvation Army to a country then ruled by a military regime. In spite of all the diplomatic cable traffic, the message did not get through that his title of 'General' did not mean that he was a military man. He was therefore greeted on arrival with full military honours and enjoyed – or not, as the case may be – a complete programme with the armed forces. Any diplomat has half a dozen such stories.

Here are three cases with more serious consequences. The first is from the tangled events before the outbreak of the First World War. The Kaiser, in many ways the driving force of events, seems to have been driven by several false assumptions. When he heard of the assassination of the Archduke Franz Ferdinand in Sarajevo he promised the Austrian Emperor his undying loyalty (*Nibelungentreu* or 'the blank cheque', as it is sometimes called), apparently supposing that the Austrians wanted merely to humiliate Serbia, whose cause the assassins supported: 'the situation would be cleared up in a week because of Serbia's backing down'. The Emperor himself – on whom the Kaiser was relying – probably did not want war, but his officials, including the military, did and the Emperor was no longer in control. There was, however, no reason for this to become a general European war unless Russia came to Serbia's aid. The Kaiser's second false assumption was that his brother monarch, the Tsar would share his reaction to the regicide in Sarajevo ('the Tsar will not lend his support to royal assassins') and agree that Serbia had to be punished. Unfortunately he was unaware of the pressures on the Tsar from public opinion: there were massive demonstrations outside the Austrian Embassy in St Petersburg. The government could not ignore such protests in a country that had already suffered one revolution and might be on the brink of another. The Tsar, like his Austrian counterpart, was not in control. The Kaiser's third false assumption was that Britain ('this hated, lying, conscienceless nation of shopkeepers') was orchestrating a plot to destroy Germany. Perhaps, if Britain had been driven by a pure doctrine of interest, this would have been a logical policy: a preventative war against potential rivals before they have the chance to become too powerful for you; and perhaps the Kaiser might have tried something similar had he been in Britain's place. As it turned out, the Kaiser was not in control either: once the mobilization had begun, he discovered that the military plan – 'unalterable', he was told by von Moltke, his Chief of Staff – was to attack France, thereby violating Belgian neutrality and ensuring Britain's entry into a general European war.

The first two misjudgements made the Kaiser underestimate the risks of confrontation with Russia; the third caused him to ignore Lord Grey's attempts to resolve the crisis. In the Russian and Austrian cases at least the Kaiser assumed that he knew his fellow monarchs well (as, up to a point, he did) and that they would behave and think as he would have done himself. But he was wrong about both monarchs – probably because he failed to understand the domestic pressures on them. These mistakes were compounded by a failure to appreciate how much was at stake for his country and for Europe.

Second, to take a modern Chinese example, the casualness with which the US Government – or rather General MacArthur – decided that there was no real risk of Chinese intervention in the Korean War remains astounding. On the US side this seems to have grown out of a belief that the Soviets were becoming increasingly cautious about the evolution of events in Korea (which was true) and that China was under Moscow's control (which was false). There may also have been some residual illusion that the 'long-standing American friendship for the Chinese people' – to quote Truman – was in some way reciprocated. The US Government had good intelligence on Moscow, but almost none on Beijing; indeed, they neither recognized the People's Republic nor were they represented there.

It was therefore heroic to make any kind of judgements at all about how China would react. Britain, which was at least represented in Beijing, came closer to guessing right: and the British Government grew increasingly nervous as US forces approached the Yalu River (marking the border with China) – not that this made much difference to US policy. But British concerns focused mostly on the view that the Chinese would be worried about the electricity they got from the Yalu valley (reflecting the bookkeeping mentality that can sometimes infect Britain's own policy-making – again, the assumption that foreigners think as you do).

In fact, Chinese concerns were much broader and were perhaps not very different, *mutatis mutandis*, from those of the United States. If the United States could decide that South Korea was within its security perimeter – in spite of apparently having ruled this out – and send troops to defend a pro-Western government there, might not China, which had given a series of increasingly explicit warnings on the subject, also see North Korea as being within its security perimeter and be willing to defend its interests with force? It seems remarkable in retrospect that so little attempt was made to understand the Chinese position. In this case it might not even have been difficult. There were, of course, several knowledgeable observers of China who had good advice to give, but they had been excluded from the policy-making process by the House Committee on Un-American Activities.

The case of Korea illustrates the second way of misunderstanding foreigners, which is simply to take no account of them. In the third example, Vietnam, the United States managed simultaneously to ignore the North Vietnamese and to misunderstand the South. In his book on the Vietnam War, *In Retrospect* (1995), the ex-Secretary of Defense Robert McNamara identifies eleven causes of the disaster. The first four are as follows:

1 We misjudged the geopolitical intentions of our adversaries and we exaggerated the dangers to the United States of their actions.

2 We viewed the people and leaders of South Vietnam in terms of our own experience. We saw in them a thirst for – and a determination to fight for – freedom and democracy. We totally misjudged the political forces within the country.

3 We underestimated the power of nationalism to motivate a people to fight and die for their beliefs and values.

4 Our misjudgements of friend and foe alike reflected our profound ignorance of the history, culture, and politics of the people in the area and the personalities and habits of their leaders.[21]

McNamara had had an earlier opportunity to learn the same lessons in Cuba where the Bay of Pigs fiasco had demonstrated that the Cubans also did not share the same thirst for freedom and democracy as the United States. Given the number of US officials engaged in fighting in Vietnam, planning US strategy, dealing with the political fall-out at home, it is astonishing how few of them were engaged in trying to understand the Vietnamese – probably no more than a handful – as opposed to trying to get the Vietnamese to do what the United States wanted. There is a striking contrast with the approach to Japan after the Second World War, when the Pentagon commissioned one of America's greatest anthropologists to write a study for them on Japanese society.[22] This shows the military at their thorough best. The three examples cited above of wars that have gone wrong as a result of a failure to understand the other side are, perhaps coincidentally, all also occasions when the military came to dominate decision-making. It may be that their lack of interest in their foreign opponents came from the view that coercive power was the only way to get results.

It is a lesson we all need to relearn: foreigners are different. They have been brought up differently; their thoughts are structured differently by the different language they speak and the different books they have read; their habits have been influenced by different schools, different social customs, different national heroes, different churches, mosques and temples; they may sometimes watch the same TV sitcoms, but the TV news still comes from a different studio and from a different point of view; their ideas of justice and legitimacy may be quite different from ours.

Of course, it is difficult enough to understand anybody. We all make mistakes and we are all taken in. Chamberlain ought to be forgiven for misreading Hitler ('A man who could be relied upon when he had given his word'). After all, many Germans got Hitler wrong too. But then Hitler and von Ribbentrop – the latter might have known better since he had spent time in

Britain – also got Chamberlain wrong. '*Was nun?*' ('What now?') Hitler is said to have asked when, against expectations, Chamberlain stuck to his word and declared war in 1939. Both sides managed simultaneously to make the same mistake, each believing that their negotiating partner was playing by the same rules as them. Chamberlain assumed Hitler was a gentleman who would keep his word; Hitler never thought for a moment that Chamberlain would keep his. Fifty years later we have just been through a similar process of wishful thinking and disillusion with Slobodan Milosevic.

Chamberlain was not alone. Stalin's misreading of Hitler and of Germany was, if anything, even grosser. In spite of warnings on every side (more than seventy of them by some accounts) and despite Hitler's manifest ruthlessness, Stalin appears to have thought that Hitler would stick to the Nazi–Soviet pact right up until the minute that the German army invaded. And he was no less wrong in his suspicions of Churchill, who he believed to be deliberately using the war to bleed the Soviet Union white. Roosevelt then proceeded in his turn to misjudge Stalin, assuming that the war-time alliance could be carried over into the post-war era and that Stalin would be willing to collaborate in Roosevelt's vision of a world of open markets managed by progressive liberal forces.

These misunderstandings were between individual men, but they were also between cultures and societies. How, on reflection, could Roosevelt have understood Stalin when he had so little idea of what the Soviet Union was like? And how could Stalin, who had never travelled outside Russia – except as a political commissar with the Red Army in Poland – know anything of the mindset of someone like Churchill, coming as he did from a different world? It is hard to believe that Hitler, Chamberlain, Roosevelt or Stalin would have made quite the same errors if they had been dealing with a fellow countryman. The same could be said of those who tried to negotiate with Milosevic. During the 1990s, Western policy-makers gradually came to understand that the Balkan leaders were not necessarily honest gentlemen, however polished the English in which they lied might be.

Does this mean we should rule out diplomacy-by-fireside-chat? Not necessarily. Personal relations and power relations are inevitably intertwined and it is better that those who hold power should know and understand one another. But they do really have to know each other. That includes some understanding of their different cultural and political backgrounds – which cannot be achieved in a couple of crisis encounters – and it also means understanding their power relationships and their political (and sometimes private) motives. Personal contact is necessary – indeed personal trust is, in the end, essential – but on its own it is not enough.

Misunderstandings of one's enemies can sometimes come about because they are trying to deceive you; but misunderstandings between friends are equally common. Britain and, perhaps from time to time, the United States too, systematically underestimated the German desire for reunification. Britain and America were not threatened by the *status quo*. For them the division of Germany and the division of Berlin was a kind of solution. It was not especially satisfactory, but everyone got used to it. Leaders such as Macmillan and Kennedy were more interested in stability than in change. De Gaulle, who had also lived through a period when his country was divided and occupied, was perhaps better able to understand Adenauer.

It is especially difficult for imperial powers to comprehend the feelings of those who have been colonized. Things look different depending on whether you are on top or underneath. Empires are interested in order; their subjects want liberty and to control their own destinies. 'But are you not free under the Empire?' the puzzled imperialist might ask. During the First World War the British deceived themselves into believing that the Arabs wanted to be ruled by Britain (they also made the classic error of assuming that foreign institutions were similar to their own and supposed that the Caliphate was an Islamic version of the Papacy). Years later, in the same region, it was a racing certainty that Eden and Nasser would misunderstand each other. Much more striking in the Suez tragi-farce is that Britain should have misread the United States so badly. But Anglo-American misunderstandings have a long history. The failure, back in the eighteenth century, of Britain's imperial parliament and government even remotely to understand their North American subjects – in spite of ties of history, blood and language – was just the beginning.

Perhaps there is a general difficulty for the powerful in understanding the outside world. First, they have less need to understand others than do the weak. If you can get your way by force why bother with the tedious and time-consuming business of trying to understand and even persuade foreigners? The strong can look after themselves – at least most of the time. The problem is, the bigger you are the bigger your mistakes turn out to be and the more reluctant you are to recognize them early on and cut your losses. Second, a large country with a big bureaucratic or imperial machine will have such difficulty reaching an internal consensus that listening to foreigners or taking account of their concerns may sometimes simply be too difficult. If you sit in the middle of a big country, in a big capital city, in a big administration, then even remembering that the outside world exists can sometimes be a problem.

Modern warfare also creates distance; at first sight it seems to make understanding people less important. If you do not even need to be near people to kill them why worry about what is going on inside their heads? Such an approach forgets that winning battles is not the same as winning wars. War is about changing people's minds or at least their behaviour. If stand-off weapons foster the illusion that you can deal with foreigners at a distance, then they are as dangerous for their owners as they are for their victims. In any case, dealing with shadowy targets such as terrorist groups requires even more intelligence and sensitivity. So does making peace. If we find ourselves efficient at war but inept at peace, then we are returning to the approach of Genghis Khan or Tamerlane.

Words as well as weapons can create distance. This is a good reason for avoiding moral or religious terminology in diplomacy: describing the world in moral terms can make it more difficult to understand others. Iran's characterization (and its perception) of the United States as 'The Great Satan' is a serious handicap when it comes to making deals. Ronald Reagan started his presidency by calling the USSR 'the evil empire', but dropped this language and the sentiments behind it as he began to develop a serious relationship with Gorbachev.

A failure to put yourself in the other person's place is bad enough. The trouble is that even when you try you will probably get it wrong, since his place is not what you imagine it to be and even his imagination is different from yours. If Saddam Hussein had understood foreigners better, he would probably not have let the hostages go in the run-up to Desert Storm; perhaps he would not have invaded Kuwait in the first place. It is not even enough to listen carefully to what foreigners are saying or to watch what they do. Perhaps Saddam Hussein heard the American ambassador correctly. The Soviet Union and North Korea may also have heard correctly when Acheson appeared to say (in a speech to the National Press Club in January 1950) that the Korean Peninsula was not within the US security perimeter – implying that the United States would not defend it. The Argentines drew the logical conclusion from Britain's withdrawal of the *Endurance*; if Britain would not even pay the costs of keeping a survey ship in the region it was hardly likely to fight for the Falkland Islands. But information and analysis is not enough. You have to understand the temper of the country and of those in power – how they will react when the chips are down. Empathy may be more important than intellect. One of the reasons for Henry Kissinger's great success in Europe and the Middle East was that, in addition to his formidable intellect, he had the background to be able to empathize with both parties.

The first thing policy-makers must do is listen to people on the ground. Reflecting on the errors of Vietnam, Robert McNamara notes: 'We might have made similar misjudgements regarding the Soviets during our frequent confrontations – over Berlin, Cuba, the Middle East – had we not had the advice of Tommy Thompson, Chip Bohlen and George Kennan. These senior diplomats had spent decades studying the Soviet Union, its people and its leaders, why they behaved as they did and how they would react to our actions.'[23] But perhaps we should go one step further and accept the possibility that we might never understand each other. Sir

Anthony Parsons, who was British Ambassador at the Court of the Shah of Iran, used to recount the anxiety he felt when the Shah decided to address a distinguished British visitor in his excellent English. If the Shah spoke Persian and the conversation went through an interpreter the visitor got a sense that he was dealing with someone from a different culture. A free-flowing conversation in English was more risky: it left the impression that the two had understood each other well and that the Shah was not very different from an Englishman.

The conventional wisdom, sometimes from supposed experts, can also turn out to be wrong. 'Centuries-old ethnic hatreds' proved to be a poor explanation of the conflicts in the Balkans; and the fighting ability of the Serbs proved to be less than memories of the Second World War suggested. Nor, so far, has the thesis of many pundits that foreign forces are always unwelcome in Afghanistan been proven true. It is important not only to be on the ground, but also to be on the ground now and not twenty years ago.

A cardinal rule for diplomacy must be to listen to local advice. This, too, can be wrong, but the chances of seeing things from the wrong angle are magnified when you are several thousand miles away. It was Kennan, the experienced observer of the Soviet Union, who finally got US policy back on track, dispelling Roosevelt's illusions that it would be possible to work with Stalin. (The famous article by 'X' in Foreign Affairs arrived just at the moment when others were beginning to see the patterns of Soviet ruthlessness more clearly.) As a precondition of local advice, a country has to be represented on the ground by someone who speaks the language and understands the political culture, who sees life there day by day, who knows the temper of the leadership and the preoccupations of the man in the street and who breathes the same air as he does. The theory that in an age of telephones, e-mail and jet planes there is no need to have representation on the ground is badly mistaken. So, one should break off relations and close down embassies only when there is no other alternative (often it is precisely when a government needs them most that the pressures to withdraw ambassadors are greatest). Not that diplomats have a monopoly on wisdom or knowledge – they, like anyone else, can make bad judgements – for example, the advice of the British Embassy in Berlin before the Second World War was poor and the US Embassy in Saigon ended up dominated by the military and giving advice that reflected wishful thinking rather than the realities of the streets and the villages. Be prepared to listen to anyone who has some kind of insight into the country and the mentality of its leadership. There is much to be said, too, for lending an ear to neighbours: they will have both interests at stake and some degree of cultural empathy. McNamara's successor as Secretary for Defense, Clark Clifford, began to have doubts about US policy in Vietnam when he observed that Thailand was prepared to commit only 2,500 men, as opposed to the half a million being sent by the United States. Perhaps the Thais knew something Washington did not.

Not all misunderstandings lead to wars; and not all wars are caused by misunderstandings. In the case of the First World War, misunderstandings played an important role. But perhaps war would have come sooner or later – either because that was what Germany wanted, as some historians argue, [24] or simply because in those days war was still a part of the culture of international relations. Yet nothing is inevitable and great historical events still depend on the decisions and sometimes on the mistakes of individual men and women. If they are better informed, if they understand each other better, they will make better decisions. Whatever view is taken of the First World War, the Second World War was clearly not the result of accidents and misunderstandings. It took place because Hitler and the Nazi Party wanted it. But here, too, if others had understood this more clearly and had been prepared to act on that understanding they might have been able to prevent it. Churchill, at least, always believed this.

Dealing with foreign governments may be more difficult in a democratic age than it was in the days of a brotherhood of monarchs, when diplomats all came from the same transnational aristocracy. On the cusp of this change, the Kaiser's belief in monarchical brotherhood blinded him to the growth of national feeling in Russia and its importance to the Tsar. The common culture of an élite who first spoke Latin, then Italian, then French has gone. Instead we have a common mass culture; but that has little to do with the way people think or react. In a world of global communications and global brands the illusion of similarity is all the more powerful. Foreigners may wear the same jeans and eat the same hamburgers; they may even speak the same global (second) language, but they do not think the same thoughts.

Maxim 2
In the end, what matters is domestic politics

In the nineteenth-century, German historians evolved a theory called the primacy of foreign policy. According to this, the state would always give foreign policy interests precedence over domestic considerations. Since the origin of the state is in the creation of a common security for its people and since the first duty of every state is to protect itself from outside attack, this idea has a certain logic to it. For much of history it has probably held true. As long as states were concerned primarily with defence, and as long as monarchs owed their position to dynastic connections and the sanction of the Church rather than to their people, relations with fellow monarchs were a matter of prime importance. For a long time, in any case, state policy was mainly about foreign and defence questions, with domestic policy coming into focus only because of the need to raise taxes to pay for foreign wars. In the nineteenth century, however, in fact just as the theories about it were being developed, foreign policy was losing its primacy (illustrating Hegel's point about the owl of Minerva).[25] Governments became more dependent on domestic support and domestic supporters – in due course, voters – were increasingly interested in domestic policy.

Today the primacy of the domestic sphere is evident in almost all countries. What keeps governments in power is politics at home, not foreign relations. In Britain no general election in the twentieth century has been won or lost on foreign policy questions and, with one or two exceptions (of which Germany in 2002 might be one), this is true of every democratic country. For undemocratic countries too, the first ambition, often the only ambition, of a government is to remain in power. Sometimes this will involve policies designed to keep the mass of the people happy; sometimes the government's attention will be focused on keeping the army happy. Whatever happens, keeping foreigners happy is always low on the agenda.

It is easy to multiply examples. The power of industrial lobbies, of campaign contributors – many countries outlaw foreign contributions precisely because of that power – and of farming and fishing lobbies is well documented. Who gets more assistance, a few comparatively well-off farmers at home or the great number of poor people in less-developed countries? The answer, of course, is the farmers: globally, agricultural subsidies are worth about ten times the value of development aid. When it is a choice between domestic and foreign interests, domestic wins. Presidents and prime ministers often listen carefully to messages from foreign leaders, but they always listen much more carefully to messages from domestic interests and from voters. A good diplomat knows how to mobilize domestic lobbies. One ambassador in London, keen to get a senior British minister to pay an official visit to his country and making little progress by the normal methods, told every British company with important business in the offing that they could lose it if the visit didn't take place. Lobbying by British companies proved far more effective than the foreign ambassador could ever have been on his own. An extension of this approach is now available in the shape of international non-governmental organizations (NGOs). If you can get Greenpeace or a similar organization on your side, they may be able to mobilize domestic lobbies abroad. This, in part, is what the Canadian government did with much success in its pursuit of a treaty banning land-mines.

Even in cases where there is apparently little domestic salience, public opinion can be an important factor. The US/China spy-plane incident of 2001 (in which the Chinese forced down a US electronic surveillance aircraft, which they claimed had violated their airspace, and then made considerable difficulties about the return of the crew and the aircraft) was on the face of things a pure foreign policy question. However, it is clear that for governments in both countries domestic opinion was a major consideration: in China, the need to keep popular anger under control seemed to be the governing motive of policy. The Chinese government's fear seemed to be that anger against the US government might turn into anger against themselves if they were not seen to respond toughly. Eventually both plane and crew were returned, the former in crates. Similarly, Britain's dispute with Spain over Gibraltar, which appears also to be a question of purely external interest, is important not because of anything to do with foreign or defence policy – Gibraltar lost its strategic significance some years ago – but because of public opinion in Spain, Britain and, of course, in Gibraltar. In the handling of the Palestine question, which has simmered close to boiling point over many years, what galvanizes Arab states is not so much events in the occupied territories as the reaction of their domestic populations. It is only when there are risks on their own streets that the leaders come forward with real attempts to solve the problem.

Some appreciation of how foreign policies play to certain domestic audiences – the Republican Right, the Left of the Labour Party, the Chinese military, the Arab street – is now a part of the normal vocabulary of international relations. The point of such references is to show how much foreign policy is subject to domestic forces. Think how different US policy would be without the Irish lobby, the Jewish lobby, the Polish, Greek or Lithuanian lobbies and no doubt many others too. The Cuban lobby has for years driven a policy of striking unsuccess – the US boycott may even have helped maintain Castro in power. Reason and interest would have changed it long ago.

Sometimes domestic considerations drive foreign policy in areas that are only remotely connected. Countries concerned about movements for self-determination within their own state look at situations abroad almost entirely in this light. China wants Kosovo to remain a part of Yugoslavia, not for any reasons of Balkan diplomacy, but because of Taiwan and Tibet. Russian policy has a similar origin. If a British diplomat discusses Hong Kong with a Spanish diplomat, the analogy with Gibraltar is never far away.

On other occasions foreign policy may be a symbol of a more deeply grounded struggle for domestic influence. This is probably the case, for example, in the foreign policy battles between so-called reformers and hardliners in Iran. The real battle is the struggle for domestic power and the foreign policy dispute is no more than its shadow. Legitimacy and therefore power derives from domestic opinion, which is concerned most with policy at home. Domestic policy is about obtaining power at home; without that there is no possibility of exercising influence abroad.

Since what matters most is domestic policy, foreign policy is of secondary interest until it begins to impinge on domestic issues. When diplomacy is about 'other people' – the situation in the Middle East, the crisis in Africa, the need to stabilize Afghanistan – it can be important and passionately interesting, even vital for long-term national interests. But when domestic interests – employment, taxation, immigration or social security arrangements – come into play, suddenly the tone hardens. These are supposedly 'low politics', the sort of day-to-day political issues that are far removed from diplomacy, but which win and lose elections. If negotiations abroad are going to result in a rise in taxation at home or an increase in immigration, then the debate becomes much tougher and more intense. In times of peace these are the vital interests of governments.

Prime ministers and presidents become engaged as much as foreign ministers. Foreign policy begins at home.

The Chinese rejection of Lord Macartney's embassy was nothing to do with foreign policy. Instead it reflected the conviction that allowing trade with the outside world would upset internal stability in China. Roughly the same kind of logic is applied, in reverse, by China's modernizers today. China has joined the World Trade Organization (WTO) not for reasons of foreign policy, but because the Chinese government believes it will shake up the domestic economy ('economic reform' is the polite term) and will increase prosperity in China. The policy might be external, but its motives are domestic. The Kaiser misjudged Russia's reaction to events in Serbia in 1914 because he was unaware of the domestic background. The moment the treatment of Slavs became a matter of popular feeling in Russia – as nationalist sentiment spread across Europe – it became a domestic issue for the Tsar and foreign policy had to take a back seat.

The point is that foreign policy is the external reflection of domestic politics: what a government's domestic priorities are, what issues arouse strong popular feelings, what makes it succeed or fail. In times of war, foreign policy is of supreme importance; but that is because the threat faced – invasion, occupation and all its consequences, including loss of property, violence and loss of autonomy[26] – would be castastrophic domestic events. For the same reason, strategic decisions about membership of alliances or other far-reaching agreements such as participation in the European Union ought to be seen as important items on the domestic political agenda, because they will have serious domestic consequences.

Since foreign policy is an external projection of domestic

affairs, it follows that real change in foreign policy comes from domestic change. One need only look around to see this. The transformation of Europe since 1989 came about through Gorbachev's programme of *glasnost* ('openness') and *perestroika* ('restructuring'), both Russian words referring to domestic political objectives in the Soviet Union. The other great changes in Europe have also come about through domestic revolutions: the end of authoritarian and military government in Spain, Portugal and Greece. Further afield, the end of the Cultural Revolution in China had a profound impact on the kind of China its neighbours had to deal with: foreign policy became less aggressive and focused on Chinese interests rather than ideological questions; it did so because of domestic events. Domestic change in Iran brought a revolution in foreign affairs – replacing an alliance with the United States with twenty years of hostility – in spite of supposedly unchanged geopolitical verities.

The Cold War is particularly important because it was, in the end, a war between competing domestic policies. To explain the forty-year struggle as being one between rival Soviet and American hegemonies misses the point. It was a struggle between two systems – democracy and the market economy on the one hand and, on the other, state control of the economy plus party control of everything else. The end of the Cold War and subsequent developments have made this clear. The defeat of one system has been followed not by imperial takeover, but by domestic change: new constitutions, membership of capitalist bodies such as the WTO and the International Monetary Fund (IMF) and privatization.

In the twentieth century, domestic matters became a dominant theme of foreign policy: democracy, human rights, treatment of minorities are all now legitimate subjects for diplomacy and, occasionally, even causes for conflict. Now that the Cold War confrontation is over, the main form of conflict is civil war and the main occasions for intervention are domestic conflicts and humanitarian issues.

Thus it turns out that some of the great foreign policy issues of the day revolve around questions such as how democracy can be introduced in Iraq without creating instability, how Afghanistan is governed, how minorities are to be protected in Bosnia and Macedonia, how the Palestinian Authority should be reformed. Those who called for 'regime change' in Iraq were a minority in the international community, but in practice it is only a matter of degree that separates them from what is now the common currency of international relations. This is not wholly new. In the seventeenth century, the central foreign policy question in Europe was whether a country would be Catholic or Protestant and, in the nineteenth century, whether it would be a monarchy or a republic. But it *is* new that issues of this kind should have become the main themes of foreign policy. In 1945, for instance, questions of whether countries such as Poland and Czechoslovakia (not to mention Germany) were going to be democratic and how and by whom they would be governed, was part of the origin of the Cold War. In recent history the systems of governance in much of central Europe, in Korea, in Vietnam, in Cyprus, in Cambodia and Afghanistan have all been subject to international negotiation. State building as a foreign policy objective began after the Second World War and, on and off, has been part of the agenda ever since.

The idea that domestic and foreign policy ought to be kept separate arises from the concepts of sovereignty and self-determination; the belief that people should be free to determine their own destiny and their own policy provided this does not interfere with anybody else. Thus, a country's foreign policy is a legitimate subject for diplomatic complaint, ultimately even for military action, but not its domestic policy, which is its own business. For a long time this separation has been one of the main tenets of the international order. It is still dear to many countries (especially those which I classify as 'modern'), in particular to those with a recent colonial past and bitter memories of what it means to lose autonomy. But it is also dear to the United States, where one school of thought, at least, insists that the US constitution is the only source of authority, domestic or international.

The difficulty is that as borders become more open – itself a consequence of a foreign policy that has brought a long period of peace – the impact of developments abroad increases. Foreign competition, the illegal trade in drugs, illegal immigration and, as we have seen, opportunities for international terrorism all multiply. These challenges on the home front have their origin in problems abroad: wars and failed states captured by corrupt or criminal interests. All require foreign policy solutions. In war, foreigners arrive in a violent and obvious way; in peace, their arrival is less dramatic and their presence less obtrusive, but the effects can be just as far reaching.

The myth persists that interference in the internal affairs of another country is somehow an aberration in foreign policy. Such interference used to take place only in unusual circumstances – at the end of a war, for instance, or when normal domestic structures had broken down. These were exceptional moments in a country's history. But with globalization all this has changed. The essence of globalization is that it erodes the distinction between domestic and foreign events. Investment decisions in Japan affect jobs in Europe; famine in Africa evokes an outpouring of sympathy in the United States (as TV images are beamed straight into American homes); Egyptian-born terrorists wait in Hamburg for instructions from a Saudi in Afghanistan to attack New York. There may, therefore, be many reasons to be concerned about domestic politics in foreign countries and even a need to intervene. As empires are replaced by weak and poorly governed states, such intervention becomes increasingly normal.

Perhaps the most important change in foreign policy has been the invention of peace as a policy goal. This profound change has come from the enormous increase in the destructive power of the military – illustrated in two world wars and confirmed by the creation of thermo-nuclear weapons – but also from the change from rural/agrarian to urban/industrial and post-industrial societies. It was Gladstone, representing the new industrial classes, who first put forward peace as a major policy platform, but it took the wars of the twentieth century, with their massive impact on civilian populations, to complete the change. The reaction after the First World War on both sides of the Atlantic was the simplistic view that pacifism, more or less disguised as neutrality, isolationism or support for the League of Nations, would bring peace. This is a little like thinking that eating brains will make you intelligent. After the Second World War an approach that was more muscular and more subtle – muscular through NATO and subtler through the European Union – incorporated the objective of peace in Europe not just into policy, but into a permanent framework.

Today Europe has moved on a stage further. In a global economy, in which the distinction between 'domestic' and 'foreign' has been eroded and in which our well-being depends so much on the open system of trade and investment, the costs of major military disruption are greater than ever before. This does not make peace inevitable – there are no limits to anger, greed and stupidity – but it does mean that the policy goals of the developed world are different from those of earlier ages. The strong preference for a peaceful environment is why intervention in other people's civil wars is increasingly frequent and why troops are trained for peacekeeping as a professional skill and why today police as well as troops are often deployed abroad. That an army – a quintessential foreign policy instrument – should take on law and order duties abroad is in some sense the final triumph of the domestic over the foreign.

In the US presidential election campaigns, domestic policies usually dominate: this is strange since the President has more influence over foreign affairs than he does over domestic matters where Congress, the Chairman of the Federal Reserve Bank and federal states are all-powerful. Even so, the world's single most important foreign policy actor is almost always chosen on the basis of domestic politics. As Bill Clinton, one of the great masters of electoral politics, put it: 'It's the economy, stupid.' For the United States, as for most countries most of the time, politics remains first local, second domestic, with foreign policy coming in a poor third.

The difficulty with this position today is that, in a borderless world, events abroad can have a powerful domestic impact – and when they begin to affect domestic affairs they become serious. Problems abroad are self-evidently someone else's problem. The trouble comes when the someone else in question is unwilling or unable to solve them. And precisely because one person's foreign policy problem is another's domestic problem – perhaps even a matter of political life and death for him – he is unlikely to take much notice of what foreigners say on the subject. The difficulty of persuading a foreign country to change its policy to deal with domestic problems it is creating elsewhere is the theme of the next maxim.

Maxim 3
Influencing foreigners is difficult

A curious thing happens to American presidents once they have been elected. As candidates they focus mainly on domestic policy, often playing up their status as someone from outside the Washington establishment. They may well have derided their incumbent opponent for spending too much time on foreign affairs. But a year or so later the President is giving an increasing amount of time to foreign policy issues. This is not just an American phenomenon. Something similar seems to occur, to a greater or lesser extent, to prime ministers and presidents in most European countries.

Reducing crime or unemployment is a difficult and uncertain business. One must negotiate with some tough domestic lobbies and, however carefully policies are planned, no one can be sure how they will work in practice. At home, progress in taking policy forward is a slow and painful process. Foreign policy, on the other hand, offers the apparent prospect of success, plus, perhaps, a little glamour. Leaders can hold summit meetings, reach international agreements, sign treaties, make generous aid commitments, even, *in extremis*, deploy armed force.

The idea that foreign policy is easier than domestic affairs is a strange illusion. Foreign policy is about that part of the world that is beyond the direct control of your government. At home governments can make laws and can, in theory at least, enforce obedience. Abroad they can only try to persuade and hope that their advice will be followed. Influencing foreign governments is not easy. Each political leader is locked into his own domestic system and the influence on them of outsiders is bound to be limited. Often a major effort is required to bring about a comparatively meagre result. Frequently, even over a long period, there will be no result at all. Look, for example, at the time and effort devoted over the years by US special envoys, Secretaries of State and presidents to the problem of Palestine. After Gulf War I, when American prestige was at its height, the Bush/Baker administration managed to get both sides to the negotiating table; and careful backstage diplomacy even got as far as a framework agreement (the Oslo process). But whether through bad luck or bad faith, implementation was continuously delayed or disrupted – this in spite of heavyweight interventions from people such as Senator Mitchell or the head of the CIA, George Tenet, acting on behalf of the President. Finally President Clinton himself embarked on a marathon negotiating process at Camp David; but this too was without result. One can blame one or other side as one chooses, but the lesson remains: even for a superpower, getting other people to do what you want is extremely difficult.

Making and implementing a change of policy is hard enough in your own country: doing so from overseas is a massive challenge. If vested interests at home can resist pressures for change from a legitimately elected government, it is even easier for interests in a foreign country to do the same, especially when they know that they will still be there long after the foreigners have departed.

Moments do come when outsiders have a real chance to exercise influence. For example, when an existing order has broken down, perhaps after a war, there may be an opportunity for a strong and well-organized power to build something new. We have seen this on a grand scale after the Second World War. (The same opportunity may present itself today in Iraq.) But the business of creating or reconstructing a state – nation-building – is much more difficult than that of destroying a regime. The evidence of Western efforts in the Balkans makes this clear. After a brief use of force and a long diplomatic negotiation, the task of constructing a Bosnian state has now gone on for several years and has cost several billion dollars. Peace and order have been restored; political life has resumed with regular elections; crime is being tackled; the army and police force are being reconstructed; but the end is not yet in sight. Nor should this come as a surprise. If it is difficult to run your own economy it is much more difficult to run someone else's; if reducing crime at home is a challenge, then eliminating organized crime abroad is a nightmare; if securing domestic reform is difficult, then remodelling someone else's country must be next to impossible.

How then should states deal with situations abroad that affect their vital interests? The question is increasingly relevant in a global era in which the actions of foreigners can impact on the domestic scene, in which developments in Afghanistan, say, or in Saudi Arabia can change lives for ever in New York or Paris. The answer is that states have at their disposal three main instruments of influence: words, money and force. They can persuade, they can bribe or they can coerce.

At first sight persuasion seems the weakest of the three. In so far as words carry weight, it is because they represent either promises of assistance or threats of violence. This implies they have little force of their own, but stand for one or other of the two instruments of influence. But neither economic instruments nor military force have an unmixed record of success.

Money has the particular disadvantage that once you have given it to someone it is hard to get it back. A continuous flow is required to maintain influence. Even so, money may not buy very much. Financial assistance is always a double-edged sword. One would think that the supply of desperately needed finance would give the IMF a lot of leverage. In practice, things are not so simple. Withdrawing assistance and provoking economic collapse is not in the donor's or the lender's interests. Setting conditions for loans may be effective while negotiating them, but getting countries to stick to the conditions they have agreed is not easy once they have the money in their pocket. A large proportion of IMF programmes are renegotiated in whole or in part.

Using economic assistance to achieve non-economic goals is even more difficult. Suppose aid is made conditional on improvements in human rights: what policy should a government follow when the country concerned pursues admirable economic policies, but fails to do anything about human rights (as in Pinochet's Chile)? Cutting off aid is a poor way of rewarding good economic management and it is unlikely to do much for human rights either. The same problems arise if you try to link aid to foreign policy. Should the international community have stopped aid to Uganda, which had excellent anti-poverty programmes, because it did not like the role the Ugandan army was playing in parts of the Congo? Using aid as leverage is something between a poker game and a game of 'chicken' for national and international stakes. The Kosovars, who are heavily dependent on foreign aid, are also very independent-minded people who frequently do not do as they are told. But is the international community going to quit? It seems highly unlikely. Sometimes donors can get quite a lot for their money if they play a tough game and if the money is released rather slowly. But they are more likely to succeed if their strategy is co-operative rather than coercive and if they can work within the domestic system. Operating with domestic allies, such as the Finance Ministry, strengthens the donor's position enormously. Above all it is sensible to be modest in one's objectives. A single focus, persistently targeted over time, is more likely to be successful than the shifting pursuit of multiple objectives.

Something similar is true of defence assistance. A government may have some leverage at the point at which it is negotiating the assistance, but once it has embarked on the programme it has a policy commitment to the country. The donor is as much at the mercy of the recipient as vice versa. The United States – in spite of the massive assistance it gave – never managed to get the South Vietnamese government to behave the way it wanted; nor has American leverage on Israel been all that its close defence relationship – some $70 billion of assistance over the years – would seem to imply. Lenin's question 'who/whom?' might be posed of this as of almost any other close relationship. Part of the explanation is that aid is rarely given just for the sake of leverage. The United States assisted South Vietnam and continues to assist Israel, because of its commitment towards them. In most cases this is more than a policy calculation that can be switched on and off; it will relate to important national objectives and, especially in the Israeli case, powerful domestic forces may be involved. Commitment to a country means having to live with whatever policies the government of the day there is pursuing.

Negative economic instruments are also a double-edged sword. Sanctions provide some incentive for the target country to change its behaviour and their removal may eventually be a useful card in negotiations. But they are likely to hurt the people rather than the rulers, who usually know how to look after themselves. In spite of all efforts to the contrary this is what happened in Iraq. Paradoxically, perhaps, sanctions will be most effective where they are least needed – against democracies – since hurting the people might cause them to take revenge on the government at the next election. Even then they can also have the perverse effect of strengthening the government. External coercion often provokes a closing of ranks even around an otherwise unpopular government. It can have other perverse effects too. In the case of Serbia, the government was not only able to blame the country's economic misery on sanctions, but it may even have profited from them since sanctions put power into its hands, through the possibility of manipulating the rationing system. A semi-criminal government like that of Slobodan Milosevic, with a good range of underworld connections, thrives in an environment of smuggling and illegality.

Sanctions do not always fail. Where they succeed it is rarely on their own but as a part of a wider policy involving other pressures or inducements. Most importantly they have to be pursued over a long period. This has been the case in South Africa, Rhodesia and Serbia – where military force and many other factors probably played an important role in bringing down the regime. The case of Libya, following the Lockerbie bombing – when there was a limited objective of getting two government employees to trial and sanctions were applied over a long period – is a good example of how they can be used effectively. But it is notable, in these and other cases of the successful use of sanctions, that the element of isolation implied by the sanctions regime seems to have been as important as the economic impact. Most people want to belong to a community and most governments want to belong to a world or at least to a regional community. Recently the trend is to emphasize this element of exclusion in sanctions in the shape of a ban on visas for the leadership, rather than economic measures that hit the most vulnerable and the least powerful. This has been tried with some success in the cases of Serbia and Belarus, but with rather less success so far in cases such as Zimbabwe or Burma (Myanmar).

Military force is the ultimate sanction in international affairs. It represents power rather than influence. The attraction of using armed force for a government is that for once it is really in charge: its own people, obeying its own orders, are going in to sort things out. For once it can ignore the awkward foreigner factor. It may be expensive and risky, but armed force does at least get results. Or does it? History is equivocal. It is not simply the fact that – at least in the twentieth century – those who have started wars seem mostly to have lost them and suffered a great deal in consequence. Even the victors have not done well in the long run. Fifty years of Soviet occupation of Eastern and Central

Europe has left little behind except bad memories and suspicion. Nor did the Japanese occupation of Korea, the Indonesian occupation of East Timor, the German occupation of Alsace-Lorraine or the Israeli occupation of South Lebanon achieve anything lasting apart from hatred. Machiavelli warns his prince that it is better to kill someone than to take their property from them – a murder may eventually be forgotten, but a theft breeds lasting enmity. Perhaps this applies in international affairs too. A defeat in a war will one day be forgotten; occupation is a cause of enmity so long as it goes on. The bitterness caused by the German occupation of Alsace-Lorraine is but one example.

Military action did work in the case of Milosevic and Kosovo – although a much longer period of bombing was required than had been anticipated. But the real change in Yugoslavia came with the domestic revolution some time after the foreign intervention. Isolation as much as military action brought the change; and the policies of Europe and the United States following the conflict in Kosovo were as important as the campaign itself: sanctions, isolation and support for the opposition. In Gulf War I, military action solved the military problem, but left unresolved the political problems of an aggressive dictatorship, a divided people and a government which, through its access to vast oil revenues, could divorce itself from them.

Short of war leading to unconditional surrender and occupation it is difficult to find many examples of problems being solved purely by military means. Even the history of unconditional surrender in the Second World War suggests that the best function of military operations is to provide an environment in which political solutions can be negotiated (a definition which applies to peacekeeping as well as to war).

Military victory was a precondition for success in Germany and Japan; but it was the policies that followed as much as the military action itself that created lasting peace. In the Balkans and in Afghanistan it is just the same: it is what you do after the conflict is over that brings stability or permits a relapse. Gulf War II has solved the problem of Saddam Hussein; it remains to be seen if it solves the problem of Iraq. That will depend on the post-military policies. Shortly before he died, Napoleon, who should have known, is reported to have said: 'Nothing permanent is founded on force.'

Perhaps there is a general difficulty in trying to achieve co-operation by means of coercion: a sullen acquiescence may perhaps be achieved, but that is not the same thing. Remove the instrument of coercion – whether it is finance or force – and you are likely to lose even the acquiescence. Compulsion usually provokes resentment more than it encourages genuine co-operation. Coercion did not produce real allies for the Soviet Union in Central Europe; force can make terrorist attacks on Israel from the Occupied Territories more difficult to mount, but it does not persuade people to give up the idea of armed struggle. Both military force and money have a part to play in changing policies, but if the changes are to stick something else is needed. And that brings us back to words.

In the end people must want the change and must have an alternative vision of how the world might be. To achieve this, the words must offer more than a promise of temporary financial help or the threat of (temporary) military coercion. To persuade political leaders to change their policies, risk their careers and gamble with their country's future requires a massive commitment on the part of those doing the persuading. But if that commitment is to a future in which that country will be included in a system which gives it a voice, a seat at the table, equal treatment and legal rights then it might just be persuasive. Not with every country on every occasion – soft words had exactly the opposite effect on Hitler and were never likely to work with Saddam Hussein – but at the right time with the right man, they are the only way towards lasting change.

The power of real commitment is illustrated by the transformation of post-war Europe and of Japan after the Second World War. (Conversely, the disastrous results of lack of commitment can be seen following the First World War.) The nature of that commitment will be explored further in the fifth section of this essay, but it is instantly visible in the US troop presence that has continued to this day in Europe and the Pacific – in contrast to the situation after the First World War. In the Balkans today one of the most powerful motives driving reform is the possibility of joining the Euro-Atlantic community. This process has already begun with all the countries of the former Yugoslavia now belonging to the Council of Europe and one of them, Slovenia, already accepted into NATO and the European Union. If Europe and the United States have begun to succeed in the Balkans it is because of the commitment to EU membership that has gone hand in hand with NATO force and EU money. This is the use of force in a constructive sense: usually we think of force as an instrument of coercion, but it can also be used to protect, to reassure, to build confidence, to include rather than to threaten.

Getting foreign governments to change their policies is difficult enough; getting factions in a civil war to stop fighting is even more so. An intense effort and a concerted strategy by the entire international community will often be required. When people are fighting it is because the reasonable ways of solving problems have already failed. The longer conflict goes on, the more passions are aroused and the more reasons there are to continue. Each soldier killed or woman raped becomes another reason. In such circumstances, where the parties cannot make peace themselves, someone else has to force them together. In some respects, making peace in these conditions resembles making war. At least some of the same principles may apply, notably those of mass and concentration. Generals concentrate their artillery and their shock troops on a single point. Diplomacy must do the same: focus on a limited number of goals and assemble the most powerful coalition possible. Finally it has to use live ammunition, to make real commitments – time, men and money. And also words – for, in the end, to persuade people, money and force can help, but vision and commitment are the most essential elements.

The importance of coalitions in making peace has been demonstrated in the Balkans. The Contact Group was the key to the Dayton agreement in Bosnia; so long as Britain and France were thought to be on one side, with Germany and the United States on the other (and Russia playing a separate game altogether), there was no hope of a solution. Each party could find a reason for holding out against a settlement on the grounds that the Americans/ Russians would come to their rescue. Only when there was external unity did an internal settlement become possible. In the case of Kosovo, also the unity of the international community was crucial. It was precisely when Russia started working with the NATO coalition that serious negotiations to secure Serbian withdrawal began. In Afghanistan the difference between the Bonn conference (where a settlement among the Afghan parties resulted in the creation of the Interim Afghan Authority under Hamid Karzai) and its unsuccessful predecessors in Tashkent and Peshawar was the presence of a united international community – above all the United States – pressing for a settlement and willing to back it up with money and military resources. In all of these cases, having all of the major powers visibly acting together was a vital step on the road to a settlement. If a settlement is ever to be reached in the Israel/Palestine problem it will only be against the background of a focused effort by a broad coalition, including the countries of the region as well as the key international players. A united international community is not easy to achieve and it is not the answer to every problem, but there is no better place to start.

Persuading anyone to change their mind is difficult. Most people, once they have made up their minds, do not change them. Sometimes the best policy may be to wait. The function of diplomacy is often to find a formula – frequently an ambiguous form of words – on which everyone can pretend to agree while they wait for something to change, perhaps the domestic situation on one or other side, which may make the problem easier to solve. When it proves impossible to find such a formula, often the best that can be done is to keep talking so that the existence of a 'process' gives everyone an excuse to wait and hope, rather than make things worse by taking action. Sometimes you simply have to wait for new people to emerge on the scene, such as Gorbachev in the Soviet Union or David Trimble in Ulster. It was the death of Nasser in Egypt that eventually brought change there, and the death of Mao that changed China.

The military equivalent of the diplomacy of patience is the policy of containment. And that, essentially, was the Western strategy in the Cold War. It was a fifty-year wait. Violent and deadly as they were, the proxy wars fought during the Cold War were nevertheless sideshows. The real battles of the Cold War were within the two sides: as the West managed, through numerous policy debates, to keep the Alliance together, and the Soviet Union tried with military coercion (and declining conviction) to do the same within the Eastern bloc. The Western victory in the Cold War was in part the triumph of coalition diplomacy. In the end, persistence and negotiation among the allies paid off. Compromise kept the Alliance together and the process of debate helped to legitimize it. One of the great diplomats of our time, George Kennan, put it like this:

> It would be useful in my opinion if we were to recognize that the real purposes of democratic society cannot be achieved by large-scale war and destruction ... I would rather wait thirty years for a defeat of the Kremlin brought about by the tortuous and exasperatingly slow devices of diplomacy than to see us submit to the test of arms a difference so little susceptible to any clear and happy settlement by those means.[27]

The most effective use of force may be, precisely as Kennan recommended, for containment: to make clear your willingness and capacity to defend yourself, while waiting for the right people, the right time, the right external coalition and the right internal domestic agenda to find a political solution. This strategy – dialogue and deterrence as it eventually became – worked brilliantly in the Cold War. It remains to be seen whether it can be applied to all of the threats of the post-Cold War world. Waiting is not a sound policy if you are dealing with an unstable power on the point of acquiring nuclear weapons. These, it must be hoped, will be exceptional cases (if not, the world is entering a new and dangerous phase). In other cases, patience remains a cardinal virtue of diplomacy. It can often be a long wait.

Much of what passes for foreign policy is a kind of game. Leaders make ringing declarations of friendship, praise the closeness of bilateral relations, agree on further visits to each other's countries, exchange parliamentary delegations, call for restraint and dialogue. Financial donations are made, but only for the appearance of doing something, to avoid getting involved. No one is really committed and nothing really happens. If one government really wants to change the behaviour of another it will need a clear focus and support from powerful allies; and all concerned must be prepared to persist over a long period.

Above all, a government needs to be committed. Real engagement begins when it is ready to give something that matters domestically – when it commits troops or opens its markets or, when it opens its decision-making institutions. Just as foreign affairs are taken more seriously at home when they start to impact on domestic politics, so foreign policy abroad starts to get serious when it commits domestic assets.

'Garbage in, garbage out,' as they say in the computer world. A superficial engagement will bring no more than superficial success. Money buys little in the long run and force leaves little behind when the soldiers are gone. Lasting results need lasting commitment. The most successful foreign policy in modern times – the transformation of Europe after the Second World War – was launched by an unprecedented commitment on the part of the United States. There was money from Marshall aid (designed subtly to influence domestic politics in Europe) and there was military power in the presence of US forces in Europe; but what mattered was the long-term policy of commitment to Europe that these represented. The United

States reversed its historical policies (bequeathed by George Washington)[28] and accepted an entangling alliance – as it did also in East Asia. In return it obtained an equally historic reversal of policy and behaviour in Europe.

Maxim 4
Foreign policy is not only about interests

When Harold Macmillan met President Kennedy in 1957 for the Nassau talks on nuclear matters, British nuclear strategy was in crisis. The United States had just announced the cancellation of the Skybolt programme, which was to have been the vehicle for the British deterrent. The issue was whether the United States should help Britain to maintain an independent nuclear deterrent, possibly by making the Polaris system available. On both sides officials were preoccupied with the Soviet threat, weapons programmes, alliance management and the logic of deterrence. Defence Secretary McNamara was questioning whether it was in US interests and the interests of strategic stability for allies to have nuclear weapons under their independent control at all. At the same time discussions were under way about creating a multilateral nuclear force, consisting of ships manned jointly by a number of allies and carrying nuclear weapons (which would, however, be under US control). This was intended to allow the Germans to participate in nuclear activity and nuclear risks without owning weapons. Strategists were beginning to write articles about game theory and to explore the logic of mutually assured destruction, flexible response and other nuclear strategies.

Macmillan ignored all of these questions. In his

presentation to Kennedy, his arguments were not about the Soviet Union, handling Germany inside NATO, nuclear weapons or deterrence. They were about Britain. MacGeorge Bundy records Macmillan as invoking Britain's history, finishing with its resistance to Nazi Germany in 1940, and saying that 'To give up [the independent deterrent] would mean that Britain was not the nation that had gone through its previous history... Either Britain must stay in the nuclear club or he [Macmillan] would resign and we would have a permanent series of Gaitskells' – presumably meaning a Britain half-engaged and half-neutral.[29]

From the point of view of 'interest', the case for a British deterrent could be argued either way. The question – as Macmillan put it – was not about interest, but about Britain's perception of itself, about the kind of country it was and the kind of country it wanted to be.

In his masterly study of India's nuclear policy, George Perkovich draws a remarkably similar picture.[30] He concludes that one of the driving forces behind India's nuclear programme was its wish to achieve Great Power status. Balancing this was a desire to demonstrate moral superiority over the world's major powers. The first of these led India to establish its nuclear programme, the second constantly to delay testing and to proceed only slowly with production for military use. Policy was driven by attitudes rather than interests. On the level of policy analysis, it can even be argued that the nuclear programme has worked against India's strategic interests: by driving Pakistan to acquire its own nuclear weapons, India may have negated the advantage it is always likely to enjoy in conventional forces. Whatever the balance of interest may have been, the implication of Perkovich's analysis is that it was not especially relevant. Policy grew out of national identity, not out of interest. (As it turns out, the calculation was wrong. Nuclear weapons have not brought Great Power status, the currency of power having changed somewhat since the 1950s. The fall of the Soviet Union demonstrated the bankruptcy of a purely military conception of power. And nuclear weapons are not seen as usable by responsible powers.)

The same phenomenon – that policy is not always determined by national interest – can be observed elsewhere. According to the normal calculus of interest, Iran should ally itself with Israel or at least take up a neutral position on the question of Palestine. Like Israel, it has a number of potentially hostile Arab neighbours – as the war with Iraq made vividly clear. Iran might have fallen back on the notion that 'my enemy's enemy is my friend'. That it did not shows that Islamic identity and solidarity are more important than state interest. The same observation might be made of some Arab countries too. In all cases, popular feeling is an important factor – even non-democratic countries must take note of it. For many Arab countries, Palestine is a domestic issue as much as a foreign policy interest, just as Israel is in the United States. Identity beats interest, just as domestic beats foreign.

This is one reason why understanding foreigners is important. If policy were the result of an objective calculation of interests, it would hardly matter whose policy it was. The real world is different. Iranians, Indians, Koreans and Serbs all have different views of themselves and each defines their interests in different ways.

The illustrations given here relate to the strategic framework. Within such a framework most foreign policy is, as the textbooks say, about interests. Once Britain had decided to be a nuclear power it acquired a series of interests – many of which were shared with other nuclear powers. Its views on arms control, nuclear testing, proliferation and its relations with other nuclear and non-nuclear powers – all followed from the basic decision to acquire nuclear weapons. Some interests come from history and geography. Others are acquired as a consequence of strategic decisions. When a country decides to become a nuclear weapon state, when it acquires foreign bases or joins an alliance, it also acquires certain interests, which thereafter form the basis of its national policy.

Once it has identified its interests, a country looks at the ways they may be promoted and at the threats to them. It tries to find out what the other side wants; it looks for allies – countries with similar interests – and considers what sort of deals it can make, how the two sides' various interests can be reconciled and compromises found. It lowers tariffs on one product, if the other side does the same on another; it will even go along with a joint policy it does not much like for the sake of maintaining a broad alliance. Or, more often, it listens politely to what the other side has to say, promises to take it into consideration, then does exactly what it intended to do in the first place.

Although interests are a second-order matter, the language of interests has an important role in international affairs. Precisely because they do not touch the core of a country's values or identity, it is easier to find common ground through a discussion of interests than if an attempt was made to negotiate values. Once a problem has been defined in terms of good and evil, there is no scope for negotiation or compromise. Compromises based on accommodation of interests will be essentially temporary, since interests can change or be redefined, but they may be a useful stage on the way to a more lasting settlement.

Much foreign policy follows the same sort of routine. Events take place elsewhere that a country does not much like, events it cannot do anything about. So it protests a bit and adjusts a little to the new reality; but the broad pattern of its national life goes on unaltered – except marginally, by the *fait accompli* which, in the end, it has reluctantly accepted. Or perhaps, having identified an important interest, it persists in rejecting the new reality until, if it is lucky or skilful, it can achieve some kind of reversal or at least compromise.

Every now and then decisions are required that compel a country to step outside the pursuit of well-defined national interests. These are the so-called strategic decisions – should it join an alliance; should it fight a war which could put its existence at risk; should it acquire (or abandon) nuclear weapons? Such decisions may be based on a calculation of interests, but they may also be decided on quite different grounds. They are decisions about ends as well as means; decisions that define interests rather than decisions that are governed by them. The question, for example, of whether to use force to acquire territory or whether preserving the rule of international law is more important, cannot be decided only by consulting national interests or calculating costs and benefits. It is not simply a tactical question: it is also about the kind of world you want to live in and the kind of country you want to be. Was it in the interests of the Greek island of Melos to fight Athens in 416 BC or for Poland to fight Germany in 1939? In 1914, was it in Belgium's interest to reject Germany's request for passage of its forces through Belgium (thereby violating the principle of neutrality on which Belgium had been founded)? Melos was destroyed and 85 per cent of the Polish forces lost their lives. The Belgians knew that there was no possibility of their halting the German army for more than a few days. The question of interests is the wrong one to ask. None of these countries was fighting as a result of a calculation of interests. They were fighting because that was the sort of people they were and they had no desire to be otherwise. Such points in history are sometimes described as 'defining moments'. It is an apt phrase. What is being defined is national identity. At such times a country may be acting out its national myth or even creating a new one. Out of this new identity flows the national interest.

In the long run countries choose their own identity. This is done through policy decisions, often arising from domestic pressures. Constitutions, commitments to international rules (such as the European Convention on Human Rights), membership of alliances or values as they are transmitted through the education system – all have an influence on national identity. In different ways, Sweden and America, India and Pakistan, Turkey and Saudi Arabia have all chosen particular identities. None of these inevitable.

In the nineteenth century, a central theme of British foreign policy was the abolition of the slave trade. From the Congress of Vienna, where this was an important negotiating objective, through the next five decades, when Britain employed naval forces (often contrary to international law), policy was driven not by interest but by a powerful domestic consensus, inspired mainly by moral considerations. Over the same period in the Austro-Hungarian Empire, Metternich's policy was defined by even deeper considerations: his central aim was to support monarchies against the threat of revolution, republican ideas, nationalism and popular sovereignty. This stance was dictated by the kind of state Austria was – a multinational empire ruled by an ancient dynasty. It was a result neither of domestic policy nor of foreign policy calculation based on the map of Europe and the balance of power; it grew instead out of history and the nature of the Austrian state itself. Later, it was the Austro-Hungarian Empire's belief that it had to prove it was still a power to be reckoned with (rather than an anachronism in an age of nation states) that led it into the First World War and its eventual destruction.

Britain faced a series of fundamental decisions in the course of the turbulent twentieth century. In 1939 the decision to give a guarantee to Poland was not merely a decision to oppose German dominance in Europe; it was also a decision – albeit unconsciously – to put the British Empire at risk. This policy was not adopted according to any rational calculation of interests. Some have argued, plausibly, that after the fall of France, British interests would have been better served through an accommodation with Hitler. He seems to have been willing to leave the British Empire alone, provided he could acquire a continental empire for Germany. The decision to continue the war came more from an instinct about the sort of country Britain was and the sort of Europe it wanted – or rather, the sort of Europe it did not want. Subconsciously, there was an admission that this was more important than any 'possessions' in India or Africa. It is the function of political leadership to define what people want, even before they may know it themselves: Churchill's policy was based not on a calculus of interest, but on a deep insight into the British people and their history.

After the Second World War came one of those periods when the international system is reshaped, in this case largely by the United States (with some advice from Britain) and by

Stalin's Soviet Union. Both sought to answer the same question: how to prevent a recurrence of war in Europe and how to avoid a resurgence of German power. On the American side, the initial decision was to promote a world of open markets and multilateral institutions in which the United States would play a leading role – a profound change in America's view of itself and its role, and of the kind of world it wanted. On the Soviet side, Stalin's solution was to rely on power, fear and the control of a cordon sanitaire. The contrast between the two superpowers was sharpest in the way in which they handled Germany. The United States aimed for a democratic, decentralized Germany bound into a multilateral system; the Soviet Union's solution was a Germany with state control of the means of production and Soviet control of the military. More widely, the United States pursued its policies through the Marshall Plan (which imposed the lowering of trade barriers among European countries), through the creation of the European Union (starting with the Coal and Steel Community) and through the international financial institutions, notably the IMF and the World Bank. (In due course, Germany and France also made the existential choices necessary to make the European Union the central fact in European politics.) The choices made by the United States and the Soviet Union came not from different interests – both wanted to stabilize Europe and prevent German resurgence – but from the sort of societies that they were. The United States pursued its goals through openness and pluralism – as an open society, nothing else would have been sustainable for fifty years; the Soviet Union used force and central control, reflecting its own nature.

Eventually the choices made by the United States and the

Soviet Union, choices of two quite different worlds and two different value systems – greed on the one hand and fear on the other, the cynic might say – came into conflict. When this happened, each side behaved – as countries do when they are in conflict – in ways that resembled each other, using force, deception and dishonesty. In spite of this, the Cold War remained a conflict between two different world-views and value systems. Starting from what were, objectively, similar goals or interests – an end to German aggression and peace in Europe – the United States and the Soviet Union developed two radically different conceptions of how the world ought to be: peace through openness and co-operation or peace through elimination of the capitalist class and military hegemony. This led to forty years of conflict and a situation in which the two sides defined their interests in opposing terms. The conflict made us lose sight of the similarity of interests; the similarity of behaviour made some lose sight of the difference in values.

After their catastrophic defeat in Second World War, both Japan and Germany reinvented themselves – and in both cases there was an important foreign policy dimension to the process. (Spain did something similar, with stunning success, following the death of Franco.) The transformation has been a remarkable success for both Germany and Japan, so that one could argue that in some (rather trivial) sense they were acting out of interest. But this misses the point. The choices each made were essentially about the kind of country they wanted to be. Interests and policies flowed from that and not the other way round.[31]

In passing, we may observe that while neither Japan nor Germany has pursued a very aggressive foreign policy, each has a considerable influence on those around them – more so perhaps than Britain or France, though both of these had a more active foreign policy in the classical sense. Many Asian countries have followed a Japanese policy of pursuing economic growth and leaving political issues to look after themselves. And in Europe the Cold War was won by the vision of a prosperous, peaceful, united continent – to which a peaceful and stable Germany made a central contribution – as well as by the military effort required by containment. Not only is identity more important than interest in determining policy when it comes to the big strategic decisions; it may also be the case that, in the long run, identity has more influence on others than foreign policy more conventionally conceived. What you are may be more important than what you do.

Questions about war and peace are emotional as well as rational. Analysts from the old (realist) school might say that the objective of policy is precisely to remove the emotional element and so to set limits to the damage which conflict might do. The trouble with this view is that it ignores the fact that nations are communities and communities are, in their essence, non-rational. The ties that bind may be historical, religious, tribal; or they may be based on shared experience and shared values. For better or for worse, foreign policy – on issues that affect the national destiny or the national identity – will reflect these factors as much as any rational concept of interest. At moments of crisis especially, it is likely that a nation will return to its roots and its myths and respond as the heart urges rather than as the head advises. These irrational forces have been harnessed often enough for war and oppression; the question is whether they can serve the cause of peace and liberty as well.

The ethical dimension to foreign policy lies not in particular decisions about this policy or that, about sanctions or arms sales. Foreign policy is full of dilemmas, compromises and ambiguities. No policy is ever perfect. Often there are no good choices. If you licence an arms sale, the arms may be used to oppress people. If you do not, a legitimate government may be threatened by a rebel movement prepared to commit even worse abuses of human rights. Imposing sanctions may give a government an incentive to mend its ways, but it may also cause severe hardship to innocent people. Supplying food aid in the Occupied Territories may help people there survive, but it also lowers the costs of occupation to the Israeli government. Food aid to North Korea keeps people alive, but it may also help keep the regime of Kim Jong-il in power.

Working in an environment of uncertainty, dealing with situations over which one has little control, trying to reach accommodations with people that one does not always understand or trust – this leads inevitably to mistakes and unattractive compromises. If ethics focuses too much on means – not using force, not selling arms – it is likely to go wrong. Keeping one's hands clean may have less desirable results. Neutrality has been conceived as a moral policy, but – as the Netherlands found in 1939 – it does not prevent war and invasion. Membership of a military alliance – though on the face of things a less peace-orientated policy – may be a more effective way of promoting peace (as the Netherlands concluded after the war). In a world shaped by armed force, there is often no alternative but to use force too. Pacifism saves consciences not lives.

But the argument that ethics do not belong in foreign policy and that everything will be for the best if all countries simply pursue their national interests also misses the point. Much more important than the question of how countries pursue their interests is the question of how they define them. Is their view wide or narrow? How do they want to shape the future? What sort of country do they want to be? What kind of world do they want to live in? These are the central questions of foreign policy and they are all essentially ethical.

Maxim 5
Enlarge the context

'What must always be accompanied by, or be made subordinate to, a different sort of undertaking, aimed at widening the horizons and changing the motives of men.'

George Kennan, *American Diplomacy*

This maxim comes from a remark by Jean Monnet, the driving force behind the creation of the European Union: when you have a problem you cannot solve, enlarge the context.

On a tactical level, this maxim is as old as foreign policy itself. Edward III, failing to obtain Flemish support for his wars against France, placed a ban on exports of wool to Flanders. This threatened the people of Flanders with ruin – weaving was their main industry – and obliged them to join him. This is a rare case of instant success for sanctions, though, as their subsequent behaviour showed, coercion did not make the Flemish reliable allies. Today such a policy is usually called 'linkage'. Every kind of linkage – sanctions, trade-offs, bargains (explicit or implicit) or broad alliances – all of these involve some kind of enlargement of the context. 'You help us on arms sales; we'll help you on extradition.' 'You give us a base; we'll turn a blind eye to your suppression of opposition.' 'You support us at the United Nations; we'll ensure you get the loan you want,' and so on.

Sometimes two countries can find a compromise solution to a problem, tackling it on its own – splitting the difference, so to speak. Border disputes, like those between Russia and China, may be settled with give and take along these lines. But this is comparatively rare. Usually there will be at least some thought for their broader relationship or for a trade-off in another field. (When diplomats plead for maintaining 'good relations', they are really saying that we may need goodwill some time in the future and creating a broad relationship may have a long-term pay-off.) In modern multilateral diplomacy it is almost a rule that problems cannot be solved one by one: sometimes it is even true that the more problems there are the better. A large number of problems offers greater chances for trade-offs. If there is only one diplomatic negotiation going on, then the outcome is likely to produce a winner and a loser – or at least a perceived winner and loser. Or it may simply never end, because there are not enough trade-offs available to give the losers an incentive to settle. The ideal situation is one in which everyone can go home claiming victory. A wider collection of problems may therefore be useful, since it allows a greater number of possible bargains. Sometimes it even makes sense to wait until you have a critical mass of problems before attempting to tackle them.

One advantage of the European Union is precisely that it brings together a wide range of subject matters, allowing member states to focus on the ones that interest them, while making concessions on the others. (There are gains from exchange in diplomacy as well as in international trade.) The original European bargain is often described – with some oversimplification – as being between German industry and

French agriculture. Today the need to strike wide bargains is one reason why European problems often end up being resolved at the summit level. It is only at this level that one can bring together the location of the Pharmaceutical Testing Office, the nationality of the President of the European Central Bank, the allocation of regional aid, policies on environment, agriculture, fisheries and a hundred other things. Each of these, difficult to settle on its own, can be handled more easily in the context of a wider package.

The principle of widening the context can also be applied on a strategic level, not just for bargaining purposes, but also to bring in other actors and to change the framework in which others make their policy. Bismarck supplies a brilliant example. Having achieved his aim of uniting Germany under a conservative nationalism, his objective was to maintain the internal *status quo* in Europe. In pursuing this, his biggest problem was the implacable hostility of France following Germany's annexation of Alsace-Lorraine (which Bismarck is said to have accepted only reluctantly and always regretted). Within the European context there was no hope of reconciliation with France, so Bismarck sought instead to enlarge the context by encouraging French imperial ambitions supporting them in their quarrel with Britain over Egypt and offering them an alliance against Britain over South West Africa.[32] This would have been a useful distraction from the question of Alsace-Lorraine, and also an outlet for French national pride and military zeal that posed no threat to Germany. It was also a way of bringing France into conflict with Britain, the great imperial power of the day. It even gave Germany an opportunity to show itself as a friend of France. This policy did not succeed, partly because it did not last (persistence remains one of the great diplomatic virtues). With

Bismarck gone, Germany too became imperialist. But perhaps it was in any case bound to fail: at street level, French people cared about Alsace-Lorraine as they never did about Egypt or Indo-China – the one was part of their identity, the other represented only their interests. It was, nevertheless, a striking attempt to deal with the problem of Europe's borders by enlarging the context to include the world of empires beyond Europe.

Churchill with the Grand Alliance and the Atlantic Charter thought naturally in terms of broad strategic contexts. Roosevelt with the United Nations and the Bretton Woods institutions also did the same. The negotiations between Britain and the United States on the creation of the Bretton Woods institutions provide an interesting case of an enlarged context. The potential tension between the US wish for free trade and the British need to retain some kind of managed system (if not the maintenance of the system of imperial preference) was resolved by widening the scope of the negotiation to bring in exchange-rate management, making the US Treasury a player as well as the State Department and creating a wider vision of economic management going beyond the traditional field of trade.[33] At the same time the alliance systems built up by America, both in Europe and in Asia, also brought a different and wider context to policy-making among European countries and in Japan and Korea. Today, too, by looking at terrorism as a threat to global order, the US government can build a broader alliance than would be achieved by focusing on a single incident or enemy. The 'vision thing' is often about seeing a wider context.

Jean Monnet's maxim can be used on the tactical level of day-to-day bargaining or it can be employed on the strategic level to create and sustain new coalitions of interests. What

Monnet himself did, some seventy years after Bismarck's attempt to solve the Franco-German problem, was to use this maxim not just strategically but also, in a sense, existentially. Strategically, Monnet's great achievement was to involve the domestic interests of the business community, who had a natural desire for cross-border trade, in foreign relations. Economics is a force for integration and for cross-border linkages, just as politics is sometimes a force for division. Monnet deliberately kept foreign ministries – which have a natural interest in the sanctity of borders and the preservation of sovereignty – away from the creation of the European Communities. The business community brought wider horizons, new cross border links and also substantial domestic lobbying power.

On a tactical level, widening the context means finding some temporary method of applying coercion or incentives; on a strategic level it means engaging larger interests. On an existential level it means transforming identity. Monnet's genius was to widen the definition of Us. He created a European context. Left alone, France and Germany would never have resolved their problems: as part of a common European project there was a chance they might. Today, grown accustomed to the normal relationship between France and Germany – part co-operation, part competition, part rhetorical declarations of eternal amity, part day-to-day bickering over mundane European issues – we have lost sight of the extraordinary nature of the achievement of reconciliation. Several centuries of wars and a hostility that was almost a part of the political culture on either side of the Rhine were ended by the creation of the European Union. 'Who is Us?' 'What sort of world do we want?' Posed in a wider European context rather than in a national setting, these questions produce very different answers.

The German question has been on the European agenda for more than 300 years. The original solution, Richelieu's creation of a weak Germany, gave way – thanks to time, Napoleon and Bismarck – to a strong Germany. The third way of a European Germany seems finally to have resolved the problem. This solution was not, however, a purely European affair. The American commitment to Europe was an essential element. Indeed the European/Atlantic answer to the German question was an American as well as a European conception. The US High Commissioner for Germany, General McCloy, argued that 'There is no solution of the German problem inside Germany alone. There is a solution inside the Euro-Atlantic World community.'[34] Achieving this involved the commitment of not just US forces and money, but also of the American future. It meant creating an American vision of a wider Western identity embodied in NATO and the OECD and Bretton Woods. For the United States this also entailed a major shift in identity. Instead of seeking to avoid involvement in European wars through isolation, it sought to avoid European wars by involving itself in the European peace. This wider transatlantic, western identity has sustained the alliance for fifty years and, so far, has outlived the disappearance of the 'East'. As Ernest Bevin understood, the Americans 'had enlarged their horizon and their understanding...of the United States to take in the Atlantic and several hundred million Europeans who live beyond it'.[35]

The remaking of the Franco-German relationship in the European context required fundamental change, not just in Germany but also in France. To demand change from a defeated country is not unusual; it was in these terms that the Versailles settlement after the First World War was conceived. For one of the victors to see the necessity of change is less expected: perhaps it helped, in this case, that France had also been defeated in the war. Similarly, in the creation of the Atlantic community it was not only Germany that had to change, but also the United States and even Britain (which until then had never kept forces stationed permanently on the Continent). Churchill's slogan, 'In victory, magnanimity,' has a practical meaning in the search for peace.

A lasting solution to the Israel/Palestine problem will require a transformation of Israel and also of the Palestinian identity, and probably a change of similar magnitude in many Arab states too. To insist on preserving sovereignty, to refuse to adapt our identity in some degree to accommodate others, is to insist on preserving the problem.

If we lived in a purely rational world, limited wars between rational modern states would end with a negotiation – an exchange of territory or money – and the result would be a reasonably durable peace. Settlements of this kind were common in the eighteenth century. The trouble is that from the middle of the nineteenth century we have been living in a world of nations and national communities. International relations have become a matter of identity as well as interest. Problems of peoples are not to be solved by balance and negotiation. Alsace-Lorraine became a defining point in the French identity after the Franco-Prussian War. Britain's so-called Irish Problem was one of identity; so, in part at least, are the problems in Bosnia, Palestine, Cyprus, Sri Lanka, Kosovo, Sudan and between India and Pakistan, China and Tibet and China and Taiwan. Such problems are not resolved by finding a balance of forces. Peace between nations is not the same as peace between states.

Peoples as well as governments must participate in the solution.

Why do countries stop fighting each other? It is not enough to say that it is through the balance of power or through fear. Why are Spain and Italy not colluding to attack France? Why is Germany not going to take over the rather weaker states on its eastern border? Why is Japan not thinking of invading Korea again? An attempt to answer these questions purely in the 'realist' terms of interests and power would miss the point.

Some conflicts have been brought to an end by the creation of a single state – as happened in the case of England and Scotland or Bavaria and Saxony. But in other cases, in Western Europe or in transatlantic relations, peace has been attained through the development of a wider sense of community (and with it the postmodern relationships between the states that inhabit such a space). Making the wider context a permanent feature of international life usually involves creating permanent institutions. Indeed, they are a defining feature of the postmodern world. If the timing is right, inclusion in such frameworks can foster a broader definition of identity. Widening membership· usually has costs and risks for existing members. Just as real foreign policy only begins when you engage domestically, so real widening of the context begins only when you are prepared to share rights and risks with those who, until then, had been strangers.

Some forty years after Monnet widened national horizons in Western Europe, Gorbachev abandoned the language of 'East' and 'West' and began instead to speak of the 'common European home' – a concept which both sides (for an adjustment is also required in the West for this to work) are now slowly turning into a reality. This will take time. Misunderstandings in relations with Russia still occur. Trust will come only slowly and with a transformation of the Russian state and society; a common identity will come more slowly still. But so long as the two sides spoke of 'East' and 'West' and, indeed, so long as they thought of themselves as two sides, the best that could be achieved was a ceasefire and stalemate. In a nuclear age, that is not enough. Only in the context of a wider vision can a permanent peace be assured.

None of this is easy. It is simpler for a country to redefine its interests than for it to redefine its identity. A state can be obliged to do the former through coercion, but not the latter. But then it is also easier to reverse that process and return to the previous definition of interests once a threat has gone away or coercion has ceased. (While the wool embargo lasted, Flanders had an interest in siding with England. Once it was removed, it reverted to its prior neutrality.) In contrast, shifts in identity change the international scenery for good; but these modifications come about only as part of a process that must involve a whole society as well as its political leadership. Very likely they will occur only after repeated conflict and crisis – as in the case of France and Germany. State structures may have to change to reflect new identities: again, this is the story of post-war Europe. Perhaps it will only be with changes of this order that the crises in the Islamic world and in Africa will find a lasting solution.

If enlarging the context sometimes solves problems, narrowing the context is often a way of creating or exacerbating a problem. In the Balkans, for instance, people who had once regarded themselves as Yugoslavs were encouraged by Milosevic, Tudjman and others to define themselves as Serbs or Croats instead. Most identities are created at least partly by propaganda, education or intellectual movements. Today in the Balkans the best hope of a solution lies not just in trying to solve the quarrels between individual communities, but at the same time in placing all of these communities within a wider European context, encouraging a broader view of identity through membership of European and Atlantic institutions. It was on the platform of becoming a normal European country that Kostunica fought and defeated Milosevic in the elections in 2000, and it was with the aim of becoming a member of the European Union that Djinjic pursued the policies that led to his assassination.

Civil wars and the disintegration of states usually involve the same narrowing of vision that we have witnessed in the Balkans. The focus of legitimacy ceases to be the state, but becomes the faction or the ethnic community, eventually the clan, the family or even the individual. Conflicts are created instead of being resolved. This process of decay into a pre-modern status can be observed today in many disintegrating African states: Somalia, the Congo and Sierra Leone, to name but a few.

'Widen the context' is not an automatic formula for solving foreign policy problems. Rather than start with a grand design, it will usually be best in peace talks to start with a narrow focus and to concentrate on some minor element or procedural question as a means of getting the parties to talk to each other in the first place and to begin to build confidence. In the majority of cases it is sensible to look for ways of conciliating interests so that the parties can live with each other and their mutual problem without coming to blows. The search for a wider context and a lasting peace will have to wait. The moments when it can be achieved are rare. Usually the time is not right, the leaders are not right or the people are not ready. Some commonality of values and political culture is probably a precondition. To find a permanent solution to problems, unusual leaders are required. In the usual run of things, those who are losing do not want to make deals and those who are winning see no reason to. The fighting might come to an end, but victory is not the same as peace. For that, magnanimity and vision are required.

In the West's dealings with the Soviet Union there have been three broad stages. For a long period after the Revolution normal relations were not possible. The Soviet picture of the world (a struggle between capitalism and communism, in which democracy was a sham to conceal from the workers the extent of their oppression, while the real forces driving events were economic) was quite different from that of the West; there was no common language; there were no common rules. The Soviets tried to foment revolution in the West; the West supported counter-revolutionary forces in the Soviet Union. At this stage, the main policy options were regime change and containment. The first having failed (in the civil war), the West settled down to the second. The common fight against fascism might have brought a change in the non-relationship – as Roosevelt had hoped – but this was frustrated by the personality of Stalin. Following the death of Stalin and the shock of the Cuban missile crisis, a process of dialogue began. The two sides still thought of each other as enemies, but were able to find sufficient common language and common interests to reach agreements – though, had either side seen a chance to achieve a decisive victory over the other, it would probably have seized it. Finally, with the end of the Cold War and a radical change in the Russian identity and state structure, there is the possibility of finding a more solid and lasting basis for peace that goes beyond the alignment of interests. To use the terms of Part I, one must contain the pre-modern or the alien; one can seek a conciliation of interests with the modern state, but lasting peace comes with postmodern integration of identity.

Conciliation of interests may bring a lull – not a peace, but a stand-off. This may be the best solution attainable at that moment, and it is by no means an easy objective. This is the diplomacy of containing conflict, limiting power and managing crisis – a necessary approach until the opportunity for something better comes. But for a lasting peace more is needed. It is the same with military action. The ephemeral nature of military success means that to make it last a political structure is required to consolidate and preserve gains. Conquerors may try to do this by proclaiming a new order: as Napoleon, Hitler and Stalin all did. In each case, however, either they did not mean what they said or – in the example of Hitler – what they proposed was so unpleasant for almost all concerned that it provoked only hostility.

In the end, durable and reliable peace depends on creating legitimacy. If peace is to last it must be acceptable to all. This is most obvious in civil wars – now the principal form of conflict in the world. Restoring law and order means restoring legitimacy. But the same is also true for the international community.

Napoleon was both right and wrong to say that nothing was founded on force. It is not power that grows out of the barrel of a gun, but destruction and disorder – as can be seen in all those countries where the Kalashnikov is bought and sold on the streets. Power, order and peace grow out of legitimacy – but this has all to be backed by force.

Diplomacy may be conceived as the art of restraining power.[36] In much of the pre-modern and modern world this remains true. Many states are inherently dangerous and their power can be restrained only by an equal or greater power. In these worlds, war remains the default option. But the emergence of a postmodern community in Europe over the last fifty years allows us to imagine that war may not be inevitable. There is an alternative to the restraint of power by another power: namely the domestication and legitimation of power.

The mark of a real international community, in which not just interests but also identity and even destiny are shared, will be that foreign policy becomes a part of domestic politics. This is already beginning to happen in Europe. It is bad politics in either France or Germany to be at odds with the other. In most European countries politicians do not like to be seen as anti-European. Even in Britain bad relations with Europe is bad politics (it was a factor in the downfall of Margaret Thatcher.) The same is true, though less decisively, for transatlantic relations.

There are those who are hostile to any such vision. Irving Kristol writes of the illusion that we are moving towards an eventual 'world community' where the defence of national interests would be 'replaced by a diplomacy aiming to reconcile the interests of all'. It is true that we are far from such a world. A vestigial community exists in the shape of the United Nations, and some working components are in place in the shape of arrangements for international co-operation in trade, transport, telecommunications and much else. But when it comes to security issues and the use of force, it is still largely a world of every country for itself. And security is the foundation of all things.

It is a mistake therefore to exaggerate the degree of order and legitimacy in the world. But it is also a mistake to believe that such a community could never exist and that we should not set it for ourselves as an ultimate and very distant goal. Such an objective may well be unattainable. But if this so then the alternative is the law of the jungle and that, with the development of technology, looks increasingly nasty. The attempt to do better is not merely a moral imperative; it may be necessary for our survival. The use of force is justified only if it contributes eventually to a more orderly and legitimate world. The creation of the European Union, following the most violent period in Europe's history, gives an indication of what can be done, but also of how difficult it is to do. As Monnet wrote at the end of his memoirs: 'the Community itself is only a stage on the way to the more organized world of tomorrow.'

The reason why Britain, France and Germany, in spite of a thousand years of antagonism, no longer consider fighting each other comes from a redefinition of Us. With this goes a sense of belonging to the same community – whether it is defined as Europe, the European Union or the West. This ultimate enlargement of the context – brought about by engaging domestic interests and by making foreigners a little less foreign – is an enlargement not just of the context, but of our definition of ourselves. Before we can begin to construct a foreign policy, we have to ask ourselves not only what sort of world we want to live in, but also who are We? The broader our answer, the more likely We will be able to live in peace.

Ever since men began in time, time and
Time again they met in parliaments,
Where each in turn, letting the next man speak,
With mouthfuls of soft air they tried to stop
Themselves from ravening their talking throats;
Hoping enunciated airs would fall
With verisimilitude in different minds,
And bring some concord to those minds; soft air
Between the hatred dying animals
Monotonously bear towards themselves;
Only soft air to underwrite the in-
Built violence of being, to meld it to
Something more civil, rarer than true forgiveness.
No work was lovelier in history;
And nothing failed so often . . .

from Christopher Logue, *War Music*

PART THREE
EPILOGUE: EUROPE AND AMERICA

The differences between Europe and America are shaped by their military capabilities: so runs a popular argument. To put it crudely, the United States is unilateralist because it has the strength to act on its own; Europe's attachment to treaties, the rule of law and multilateralism comes from weakness and wishful thinking. Rules exist to protect the weak and Europeans like them.

During the Cold War these differences were concealed. Europe was the battleground and the prize in the Cold War. Because of this it had an importance that exceeded its military strength. The Cold War was a contest between alliances and also a struggle between different conceptions of legitimacy: liberty was the central value on the one side, equality on the other (at least in theory). Those who are fighting on the side of liberty can hardly coerce their allies, so multilateral, consensual decision-making became as much a part of the Western ideology as free markets. During the Cold War Europeans had strategy thrust upon them. When it was over many of them took a holiday from it. Their great crisis past, European countries cut defence budgets and left the business of running the world to the United States. As the United States has taken up this offer, the Europeans have taken to complaining about unilateralism. But having neither ambition for power, nor a wish to return to power politics, they confine their interventions to declarations, treaties and a certain amount of peacekeeping after the United States has used military power.

This is a crude and over-simplified version of the argument in Robert Kagan's *Paradise and Power* (Atlantic Books, 2003), a book that has stimulated discussion in Europe and America. It is not true that Europeans have no military capability – after the United States and Russia there are not many countries that are on a par with the European Union's collective forces. Nor is it true that the Europeans are unwilling to use force. After all, it was Anglo-French artillery (in the form of the Rapid Reaction Force) rather than American bombing that made the difference in Bosnia; and it was the British and French who were willing to send in ground troops when the air campaign in Kosovo seemed to be going nowhere. (Almost all of the weather aircraft and precision munitions, not to mention the communications and intelligence satellites were, however, American.) And Germany – in spite of its long-standing reservations about the use of military force and the domestic controversy it provokes – has been active militarily in Kosovo and Afghanistan, in a way that would have been unthinkable ten years ago. Nevertheless, European capability for intervention abroad is severely limited. Only the United States could have mounted the campaign in Afghanistan (small though the forces it deployed were), let alone the campaign in Iraq.

It is also true that, as in the Balkans, as in Afghanistan (and probably in Iraq too), the United States may be able to fight wars on its own, but it still needs help from others to maintain the peace.

For all these qualifications, however, the basic facts are compelling. The most striking feature of the world today is US military dominance. And the contrast between US military capabilities and Europe grows wider all the time. It is true that most European countries are ending conscription and are concentrating on more professional, more mobile forces. But the fruits of these changes will be some time coming. Meanwhile the United States is transforming its methods of military operation even more quickly. Quite soon even Britain and France, the most capable of the Europeans, may have difficulty operating with their US allies in the so-called digital battlespace.

It is not just that the United States spends twice as much on defence as all of its European allies together, but it spends much more efficiently. The point is the European allies do *not* spend together – instead they achieve the worst of all possible worlds by spending separately on equipment that duplicates capabilities, but is rarely interoperable (British aircraft cannot take off from French carriers, to cite just one example). Consequently they achieve neither the concentration of power nor the economies of scale that the United States does. And defence capability is all about scale and concentration.

In a technological age, military spending on research and development (R&D) and on equipment gives the best indication of capability. The table below gives some impression of the capability gap – though it understates it, since adding national capabilities together gives a result much less than the arithmetical total implies. Duplication, separate military establishments and lack of inter-operability mean that the whole is much less than the sum of its parts.

Military Spending on Research and Development and Equipment in $ millions

Country	R & D	Equipment	Total
Ireland	0	50	50
Denmark	1	224	225
Belgium	1	233	234
Austria	10	323	333
Portugal	4	366	370
Finland	8	618	626
Spain	174	1,062	1,236
Greece	26	1,378	1,404
Netherlands	65	1,341	1,406
Sweden	103	2,114	2,217
Italy	291	2,291	2,582
Germany	1,286	3,389	4,677
France	3,145	5,450	8,595
UK	3,986	8,597	12,586
USA	39,340	59,878	99,218

Source: *The Military Balance 2001–2002*
(International Institute for Strategic Studies, 2001)

Nor is the difference between Europe and America simply a matter of the decline of defence budgets in the last decade. There is a general unwillingness in Europe to see the world in terms of power relations. In Germany, Italy, Greece and Spain the use of military power has – for good historical reasons – low legitimacy. And, for equally good historical reasons, most European countries would prefer to live in a world of law rather than one of power. During the Cold War these differences were sometimes evident in European pleas for engagement with communism, compared to the US willingness to adopt a more confrontational strategy. In most of the Cold War quarrels – the gas pipeline to the Soviet Union, for example, or missile deployment or development, or whether one should take Gorbachev at his word – the Europeans argued for a softer approach, relying on contact and dialogue, and the United States for a more robust military stance. As it happens, those arguing for engagement during the Cold War turned out to be right. But this does not mean that engagement is always right.

As Robert Kagan says, during the Cold War the differences were tactical: there was fundamental agreement on the threat posed by the Soviet Union, the question was how, precisely, to handle it. In the post-Cold War world, threats are much harder to identify and analyse. This is apparent when it comes to dealing with problems such as weapons of mass destruction or countries like Iraq. Unless there is a strategic consensus on the threats, their priority and, broadly, how they should be tackled, differences and disagreements between allies are likely to be much more serious. Indeed, the question will eventually arise whether there is an alliance at all.

There is some truth in the proposition that to a man who has only a hammer every problem looks like a nail. And it may be true that lack of military capability encourages European countries to seek non-military solutions. But that is too mechanistic (if not Marxist) an explanation. Europe may have chosen to neglect power politics because it is militarily weak; but it is also true that it is militarily weak because it has chosen to abandon power politics. The

European Union started as a project to make the politics of force and threat impossible in Western Europe. That was the central objective of the European Coal and Steel Authority, the forerunner of the European Union. For a thousand years foreign policy in Europe had been about alliances, conflicts and the use of force – Britain against France, France and Russia against Germany, a general alliance against the Hapsburgs and so on. The European project therefore amounted to nothing less than the abandonment of foreign policy within the European continent.

After a century in which the European state system produced conflicts of catastrophic proportions, it is not surprising that European countries value an environment in which states operate within a legal framework and conflicts are settled peacefully. The desire to spread this to the rest of the world is both natural and praiseworthy. The escape from power politics has brought great benefits to Europe. Unfortunately it has also brought illusions. Some of these were visible in the early days of the Balkans conflict, when some in Europe seemed to believe that peace and justice could be achieved by simply asking people to be reasonable.

Today it looks as though the rule of law and the peaceful resolution of disputes can be brought back to the Balkans. But they have been brought there by military power.

The same illusion is shared by those who speak of Germany or Europe being a 'civilian power'. It is true that the post-war peaceful Germany has in many ways been a model for other countries; and its transformation had a profound and beneficial effect on the continent as whole. It is also true that Europe has concentrated primarily on non-military instruments of influence in the form of financial and treaty-based relationships. In the military sphere it has concentrated rather on peacekeeping, where military force is used defensively to protect and maintain order rather than to defeat an enemy. Europe seems, therefore, to be a model of non-military power, influential but disinclined to use force. But behind every law is a policeman ready in the last resort to employ physical force. Behind every constitution stands an army ready to protect it. And behind the peaceful development of Europe in the second half of the twentieth century there has been NATO and American military power.

The Alliance and in particular the US readiness to use nuclear weapons allowed the Europeans to operate according to new rules. They limited defence spending, developed transparency and gradually created a body of law and institutions to regulate relations among themselves – the whole apparatus of postmodern security. But the outer boundaries of this system were always protected and are still protected today by military force. Behind the Constitution, which the Convention and President Giscard d'Estaing proposed in June 2003, stands an army. But it is an American, not a European army.

Perhaps this does not matter. No one is planning to invade the European Union. An EU constitution would function no better or worse without a US military presence in Europe. But the test of a country or of a community of states like the European Union is not whether it functions in easy times, but how it performs in a crisis. Even outside the context of a major threat to Europe the lack of credible force means that when it comes to questions like Kosovo, Iraq or Afghanistan the key decisions are taken in Washington. If the world were to take a turn for the worse, if missiles and weapons of mass destruction became a real and present threat to the lives of Europeans, they would find themselves highly dependent on American goodwill.

In this postmodern paradise (as Robert Kagan calls it) it has been easy to forget that force matters. Unfortunately it matters more than anything else. Soft power is useful. Development aid does good and when strings are skilfully attached, it brings some influence; trade agreements are useful ways of binding countries together and provide some leverage during negotiations. But foreign policy is about war and peace, and countries that only do peace are missing half of the story – perhaps the more important half.

In the Balkans, fairly or unfairly, the United States probably has more influence than the European Union. The European Union contributes more money, it has more soldiers on the ground (approximately three times as many in Bosnia), it offers trade concessions and, in the long term, promises EU membership. But all these pale before the guarantee of security that is implicit in the US commitment, and which is trusted by the weakest and most fragile states in the region. The United States is still seen as a great power in the traditional mould. The European Union is not. It is power that makes troubled countries feel secure, not goodwill.

Similarly, in Afghanistan, it is the United States that calls the shots, though here, too, the European Union now has more troops and gives more aid. But the real muscle when it comes to security is American. Where violence is still close to the surface, as it is in Afghanistan or in the Balkans, it is natural that military power should weigh heavily. But even in calmer regions, military force still counts more than softer forms of power. Europe may give more aid to India, but the United States has more influence. The world is an uncertain place and everyone would prefer to know that in a crisis they will have the backing of the world's only superpower. Those European governments that supported the United States in Gulf War II – in the face of serious doubts expressed on the domestic front – did so because they thought that, ultimately, their own security depended on the United States. Secure as they might be, it is impossible to guess when help might be needed. It is not an accident that the countries of Central Europe, being more vulnerable, tended to be most loyal to the United States. Power has an attractive as well as a coercive force.

Yet the idea of a single country having unrestrained and unrestrainable power is not welcome. However admirable the United States may be – and for many it is the embodiment of freedom and democracy – would those qualities survive a long period of unilateral hegemony? Since no country or combination of countries can take on the United States in a conventional war, a growing number of countries or individuals will decide that, rather than endure a world in which the rules are imposed by an alien power, they will attack the United States by unconventional means – the images of 9/11 will remain a powerful force in the minds of the disaffected. What sort of a world would we find ourselves in if the United States were both the only military power that counted and at the same time subject to continuous terrorist attacks? All-powerful and all-vulnerable? How long would the values that Europe and America share survive? Already people are held without trial or access to the law in Guantanamo Bay and there is talk in some sections of the US media about the legalization of torture.

Our domestic systems are designed to place restraint on power. Checks and balances are the most famous feature of the US constitution. It is reasonable that liberal states should pursue the same objectives in the international sphere. Restraint on US power through the existence of some equivalent and hostile power is inconceivable for the foreseeable future and anyway is not desirable (otherwise, what was the point of winning the Cold War?). Pleas for multilateralism by European countries may be the last resort of the weak or they may reflect a nostalgia for Cold War days when Europe was at the centre of a global struggle in a world in which there was still some military balance. But they are also more than this. Multilateralism and the rule of law have an intrinsic value. We value pluralism and the rule of law domestically, and it is difficult for democratic societies – including the USA – to escape from the idea that they are desirable internationally as well.

In Europe, as Robert Kagan argues, these ideals have a particular resonance. Behind them lie two world wars and more than sixty million dead, a continent in ruins and divided, morally bankrupted by fascism, collaboration and murder. There is a passage in *On the Genealogy of Morals* (1887) that illuminates this point. In a discussion on the origins of justice Nietzsche writes: 'Ah reason, solemnity, mastering of emotions, this dismal thing called reflection, all these privileges and splendours man has: what a price had to be paid for them! How much blood and horror lies at the basis of all "good things"!'[37]

Nietzsche is arguing that justice originates not in the desire of the weak for protection, but in the tragic experience of the strong. The same argument could be applied to peaceful, postmodern systems of international relations. Whatever the truth of Nietzsche's insight into the origins of justice, it is certain that the trauma of the twentieth century lies behind what might be described, in Nietzschean terms, as the loss of Europe's will to power.

What makes transatlantic relations particularly difficult today is that with the trauma of 9/11 the United States has rediscovered its will to power. The United States has always had unmatched military capability, but since the terrorist attacks on New York and Washington it has acquired a new determination to use it in defence of its homeland. The United States has always had an unwavering self-confidence in the righteousness of its cause. Franklin Roosevelt once suggested to Winston Churchill that after the Second World War every nation should be disarmed except the United States. (We may now be approaching a similar end-point by a different route.) The belief that what is good for America is good for mankind has always been a guiding conviction in Washington. But since 9/11 the United States has acquired a steely determination that frightens even some of its friends. The gap between Europe and the United States is not just about capability: it is also about will.

It is time that Europe reviewed its position. It is unsatisfactory that 450 million Europeans rely so much on 250 million Americans to defend them. There is no such thing as a free defence. No one yet knows exactly how or when, but at some point Europeans will find themselves paying for these arrangements. There is no guarantee that American and European interests will always coincide. If Europeans do not like the US National Security Strategy they should develop their own rather than complain about it from the sidelines. Better still, they should develop a joint strategy. But there is no use in having a strategy unless you have the forces to implement it. And the United

States will be interested in a joint strategy only to the extent that the Europeans bring some assets to the table.

There is a profound asymmetry in European and American attitudes to the idea of a common defence. Most European countries would state without hesitation that NATO is at the heart of their defence policy. This is more than lip-service: many countries send their best officers to serve in the NATO headquarters at Mons, most organize their military around NATO concepts, standards and procedures. Germany has foregone having its own General Staff in favour of NATO staff. Against this the US National Security Strategy sets out the ways in which NATO needs to improve its capabilities, command and control, and then says 'If NATO succeeds in enacting these changes, the rewards will be a partnership as central to the security and interests of its member states as was the case during the Cold War.' These conditional propositions are practical and reasonable, but they suggest a view of NATO as a means to an end, an instrument of policy that one can take or leave as one chooses ('The mission defines the coalition,' as the US Defense Secretary has put it). This is different from the fundamental, almost existential commitment to NATO of many Europeans and, in earlier times, many Americans.

Europeans may be capable of territorial defence, but that is increasingly irrelevant in today's world. Homeland defence begins abroad – in areas like Afghanistan and Iraq. It was easy to maintain a continuous consensus with the United States (but in retrospect not that easy) when there was a common, visible menace focused on European territory. It will be much more difficult to work together well in a world of more shadowy and more distant threats. How the United States handles the different problems of the

Middle East may have as much impact in Europe as across the Atlantic. If Europeans want to influence the United States they must bring something to the table – and that means military capability.

In general, monopolies are undesirable. One exception to this rule is the monopoly of force. This is not just desirable; it is the essential basis of order in the state and in the state system. What is wrong, then, with a virtual monopoly of force in the world? The answer is that the state is based on the *legitimate* monopoly of force and the difficulty with the American monopoly of force in the world community is that it is American and will be exercised, necessarily, in the interests of the United States. This will not be seen as legitimate.

Legitimacy is as much a source of power as force. Force without legitimacy is tyranny – for those who are subject to it. In an age in which security will depend on taking early action against emerging threats abroad, legitimacy is more important than ever. And, like it or not, the United Nations remains the most powerful source of legitimacy for such action. The proof of this is in the many failures the United Nations has survived. Success needs no legitimation, but to survive failure after failure and still attract loyalty requires special qualities. Napoleon put his finger on it when he said that the king could be defeated any number of times and still remain king; Napoleon needed to be defeated only once to cease being Emperor. The difference between them was one of legitimacy.

For the moment the United Nations remains the primary source of legitimacy in international affairs. The evidence of opinion polls suggests that this is as true in America as it is in Europe. This need not always be the case. At a certain point, if the failures of the UN system – for example, the failure to agree on necessary action in the Security Council – appear to threaten people's security, they will look elsewhere for legitimacy. Those who want pluralism and multilateralism to survive have a duty to make the United Nations effective (as the leaders of the democracies strikingly failed to do in the case of the League of Nations).

Multilateralism – for which the European Union stands and which is in some way inherent in its construction – is more than the refuge of the weak. It embodies at a global level the ideas of democracy and community that all civilized states stand for on the domestic level. But multilateralism, if it is to be effective, needs to be backed by strength, including armed strength. If the European Union cares about the multilateral system, it must do more to support it.

The idea is not that Europe should attempt to equal the United States in military power. That project is wholly unrealistic (and, *inter alia*, it would entail increases in defence spending in every European country except Greece, the creation of something like a European army, so that all planning and purchasing would be done in common, plus a long period of spending *above* US levels to overcome a technology and equipment gap of fifty years). But it could do much better than it does at the moment. Europe could even achieve this without large increases in defence spending. Suppose all European armies used the same helicopter. It would not matter if the helicopter were German/French or British/Italian; it would not even matter if it were American. The strength of buying power of the combined European defence establishment would ensure that the helicopters were much cheaper; pooling spares and sharing training would save further large sums of money and the possibilities of operating together would be vastly improved. Individual defence establishments would lose some control over the choice of their equipment, but the gains they would make in terms of costs and efficiency would more than offset this. This example could be repeated across the whole spectrum of arms and capabilities.

Good equipment is critical to military success, but the use of force is not just about equipment. To be effective, European forces would have to develop experience in operating together: that implies mutual confidence at the military and political level. And it is just as important to do peace well as it is to win wars. Here the European Union has potential (and money), if it can learn the right lessons from the Balkans. When the job of hard power has been done, soft power is critical to achieve the long-term objectives of war.

If a higher degree of integration of European forces brought both greater interoperability and greater deployability, and if this could be combined with genuinely integrated policies (as is beginning to be the case in the Balkans), Europe would go some way to answering Robert Kagan. The possibility of deploying European force would have an impact on relations with the United States. It would also make a difference to European foreign policy. Where there is no possibility of following up words with deeds, words are often irresponsible. European military capabilities would bring a more serious European approach to foreign policy. Precisely as Robert Kagan argues, power brings responsibility.

In the course of the twentieth century, Europe and the United States have exchanged positions. In the first part of the century the United States had limited military power, eschewed power politics (except in Central America) and was attached to legal concepts. European countries indulged in arms races, *realpolitik* and started two world wars. About fifty years ago George Kennan, speaking of the United States foreign policy, said:

> I see the most serious fault of our past policy formulation to lie in something that I might call the legalistic-moralistic approach to international problems... It is the belief that it should be possible to suppress the chaotic and dangerous aspirations of governments in the international field by the acceptance of some system of legal rules and restraints... It must stem in part from the memory of the origin of our own political system – from the recollection that we were able, through acceptance of a common institutional and juridical framework, to reduce to harmless dimensions the conflicts of interest and aspiration among the thirteen original colonies and to bring them all into an ordered and peaceful relationship with one another.[38]

Change the reference to 'the thirteen original colonies' to 'the six original member states' and Kennan could be speaking today about the European Union. If the United States can change so much in fifty years, so can Europe. However, it is neither desirable nor likely that the European Union will completely abandon its desire to solve problems by negotiation and by legal means. The member states are not likely to fuse on to a single state, as the thirteen colonies eventually did. Multilateralism and the rule of international law will remain essential elements in the European Union's existence. This is no bad thing. The objective of a world ruled by law rather than force, though unattainable in the short term, should remain a long-term goal. But it should not allow wishful thinking to become a substitute for the tough-minded policies required to deal with a world containing gruesome threats, including, perhaps, threats to civilization itself.

The most desirable goal would be to extend the postmodern world ever wider, so that eventually it became the norm for relations between countries to be governed by law and negotiation, so that domestic and foreign policies became intertwined and identities fused into a sense of a wider international community. This is, at best, a very long-term vision. It is probably more of a dream than a realizable goal. But even if it were achievable (and one should never rule out the possibility of things going right: who would have guessed at the transformation of Western Europe after 1945 or Eastern Europe after 1989?), it will depend on a thousand factors beyond the control of Western countries. The kind of changes needed cannot be purchased, nor can they be forced by coercion on an unwilling world. But it will not do to just wait and hope. The risks of the spread of weapons of mass destruction and the breakdown of state structures are too great. Those who want to have a chance of surviving an uncertain future should think in terms of arming and organizing to face it, while at the same time working for lasting political solutions. In a dynamic world the worst policy is to do nothing.

The logic of European integration is that Europe should, sooner or later, develop common foreign policy and a common security policy and, probably, a common defence. But the world does not proceed by logic. It proceeds by political choice. None of this will happen unless Europe's leaders want it and choose to make it happen. President George W. Bush has directly explained why we should want it. Speaking to the American Enterprise Institute in February 2003, he said: 'We meet here during a crucial period in the history . . . of the civilized world. Part of that history was written by others. The rest will be written by us.' If we want that 'us' to include Europe, we shall need more influence with the United States. And that means we shall need more power, both military power *and* multilateral legitimacy.

NOTES

1   I have many times regretted the choice of the term 'postmodern', since it carries a lot of complicated baggage that I hardly understand. It does, nevertheless, hint at the newness and complexity of the phenomenon I want to describe and especially at the fact that for the postmodern state as for the individual identity is a matter of choice – in the end, the most important feature of the postmodern state and the postmodern peace.

2   This was a popular cause in Germany, but also became one in France and remained so for forty-seven years.

3   Bismarck made this point most vividly in his famous remark 'Here lies Russia and here lies France, and we are in the middle. That is my map of Africa.' Quoted in A. J. P. Taylor, *The Struggle for Mastery in Europe: 1848–1918*: (Clarendon Press, Oxford, 1954), p. 294.

4   *Scaramouche* (1952, Dir. George Sidney).

5   For an excellent general description of the pre-modern state see Ulysses's speech in Shakespeare's *Troilus and Cressida* (1601–2):

> 'Force should be right; or rather, right and wrong –
> Between whose endless jar justice resides –
> Should lose their names, and so should justice too.
> Then every thing includes itself in power,
> Power into will, will into appetite;
> And appetite, an universal wolf,
> So doubly seconded with will and power,
> Must make perforce an universal prey,
> And last eat up himself.'
>
> (Act I, Scene 3, ll.116–124).

6   I am not alone in choosing this terminology. See, for example, Christopher Coker's 'Postmodernity and the end of the Cold War' in *Review of International Studies* (July 1992), or Stephen Toulmin's *Cosmopolis: The Hidden Agenda of Modernity* (University of Chicago Press, 1990).

7   The Prisoner's Dilemma is the name given to a class of problems in game theory. This mathematical discipline, conceived originally by Johnny von Neumann in the 1950s and 60s examined the strategies to adopt in situations where there were several participants with conflicting objectives and limited information. Game theory was developed in particular by Rand Corporation and was used in the development of nuclear strategy. A typical example of the Prisoner's Dilemma involves two prisoners held separately and questioned about a crime they are suspected of having committed together. If they both remain silent they go free. If one remains silent but the other gives evidence against him, the first receives a severe punishment and the latter is rewarded. If both give evidence against the other, they are both

NOTES

punished. (There is some analogy here with the situation of a nuclear power considering the possibility of a surprise attack.) Such problems have no solution. The dilemma arises because of incomplete information. If the two prisoners can break out of their isolation and create a joint strategy, they can together obtain the best outcome. This in effect is what the two sides of the Cold War have succeeded in doing.

8 Association of South East Asian Nations.

9 North American Free Trade Area.

10 Mercado Commun del Sud (South America).

11 The African Union.

12 Strategic Arms Reduction Treaty.

13 Anti-ballistic Missiles.

14 Perri 6 of Demos commented on this paragraph: 'The rise of individualism is coincident historically with the rise of organizations. Cultures of individualism are arguably sustainable only in a highly organized society: individualism is not self-sustaining or victorious over other principles of social order.' I agree: this is a useful corrective to balance my possible over-statement. The complex organizational structures that are necessary to sustain individualism coincide exactly with my own picture of the postmodern state.

15 The phrase was, in fact, used by President Bush in the context of Gulf War I.

16 The former Yugoslavia contains elements of pre-modern, modern and even postmodern. It used to be pre-modern (hegemony option); this has dissolved and it is trying to escape from chaos into the modern national state. In Bosnia, there are many with postmodern longings.

17 Speech to the Chicago Chambers of Commerce in September 1998.

18 Henry Kissinger, 'Has NATO's success heralded its own demise?' (1999).

19 Henry Kissinger at the 'Britain in the World' conference (29 March 1995).

20 The classification of states as pre-modern, modern and postmodern is explained in detail in the previous essay in this book. The pre-modern state is not really a state at all: it is an area of chaos in which the Government has lost its monopoly on violence, where civil war and criminal activity make life a daily nightmare – as is the case in Somalia or a number of other places in Africa. The modern state is the most familiar: driven by nationalism, sometimes aggressive, insistent on its sovereignty and on its monopolies on law and force, it has been the main constituent of the world order for a hundred years or more, as well as the most dynamic and sometimes the most violent element. The postmodern state is prepared to redefine its sovereignty as legal rights and to accept mutual interference in internal affairs; the prime example of a postmodern community is the European Union.

21 Robert McNamara, *In Retrospect: the Tragedy and Lessons of Vietnam* (Times Books, 1995)

22 Ruth Benedict's study, *The Chrysanthemum and the Sword: Patterns of Japanese Culture* (Secker & Warburg, 1947) remains a classic to this day.

23 Robert McNamara, *In Retrospect* op. cit.

24 The most well known being Franz Fischer in *Germany's War Aims in the First World War* (London, 1967).

25 Hegel refers to the fact people often only become conscious of a phenomenon at the moment when it is about to disappear.

26 Loss of autonomy has a real effect on daily life. For instance, in Occupied Germany, Allied directive No. 1 stated that the official languages in Germany were henceforth to be English, Russian and French.

27 From a lecture 'International Council of Atomic Energy' given by George Kennan in 1949; quoted in John Lewis Gaddis, *Strategies of Containment: A critical appraisal of postwar American National Security Policy* (Oxford University Press, 1982).

28 Washington's farewell address to Congress includes a famous passage in which he says: 'Our detached and distant situation invites and enables us to pursue a different course [from that of alliances] ... Why, by interweaving our destiny with that of any part of Europe, estrange our peace and prosperity in the toils of European ambition, rivalship, interest, humour or caprice? It is our true policy to steer clear of permanent alliances with any portion of the foreign world, so far, I mean, as we are at liberty to do it.'

29 This incident is recounted in Richard E. Neustadt's *Report to JFK: the Skybolt Crisis in Perspective* (Cornell University Press, 1999). Two other points relevant to this essay are of interest. First, Macmillan explicitly ruled out withdrawing America's base facilities at Holy Loch – rightly so: friendship always buys you more than threats. Second, Neustadt concludes that the United States devoted insufficient effort to trying to understand its closest friends: 'Had London been Moscow, the Kremlinologists would have come out in force.' But there were no Whitehallologists. Neustadt's book, as a whole, is an eloquent argument for the need to put serious effort into understanding one's allies as much as hostile states.

30 George Perkovich, *India's Nuclear Bomb* (University of California, 1999).

31 According to the existentialist school of philosophy, 'existence precedes essence'. In foreign policy one might also say that identity precedes interest.

32 See A. J. Taylor, *The Struggle for Mastery in Europe* (Clarendon Press, 1954), chapter XIII.

33 See John Ikenberry, *After Victory* (Princeton University Press, 2001) pp.188–90.

34 Ikenberry, *After Victory*, op. cit. p.198.

35 Ibid. (from a report by Lord Franks) p.264.

36 This remark is from Henry Kissinger's brilliant book, *A World Restored: Metternich, Castlesearch and the Problems of Peace, 1812–1822* (Weidenfeld & Nicolson, 1957). The oddity is that Kissinger goes on to underline that Metternich's great achievement was in persuading other European countries to accept his value system. Perhaps Kissinger's point is that power is restrained, above all, by legitimacy. If so, then he is as much a neo-idealist as I am.

37 Friedrich Nietzsche, *On the Genealogy of Morals* (Cambridge University Press, 1994).

38 George F. Kennan, *American Diplomacy* (University of Chicago Press, 1957), p.96.

INDEX

INDEX

colonization, 68–9
communism, 52–3, 55, 86, 159
Congo, *see* Democratic Republic of Congo
  (DRC)
consumerism, 51
containment, 87, 124–5, 136, 148
Convention on Torture, 31
Council of Europe, 38, 41, 44, 122
crime, 66, 77, 115
Croatia, 59
Cuba, 93, 99; US boycott, 105
Cuban missile crisis, 84, 148
Cyprus, 72, 109, 144
Czechoslovakia, 109

Dante Alighieri, 7
Dayton agreement, 84, 123
De Gaulle, Charles, 96
democracy, 14, 25, 32, 48, 69, 93, 108, 168
Democratic Republic of Congo (DRC), 66,
  147
diamonds, 67
diplomacy, 84, 96, 100, 106, 123, 124–5, 139,
  149–50
domestic policies, 27, 29–30, 31, 102–13,
  114, 150, 151, 171; intervention in, 3–4,
  59
dominions, 33
drugs, 66, 67, 110

East Timor, 71, 120
economy, 51; postmodern, 79
Eden, Anthony, 97
Edward III, King, 138
EFTA (European Free Trade Association), 33
Egypt, 124, 141; financial crisis, 71
empires, 7–8, 7–9, 11–13, 14, 17, 24, 69–70,
  76, 97; colonial, 19, 20; and religion,
  18–21; voluntary (co-operative), 70, 73,
  78–9
England, 24, 145, 146; civil war, 8
Enlightenment, 52, 86
ethnic cleansing, 59
Europe: security system, x, 5, 43, 53; balance
  of power, 3, 4–6, 9–12, 14, 16, 35, 69; state
  system, 4, 8–9, 11, 21, 69, 160; leadership,
  6, 8; empires, 11–12, 16; wars of religion,
  21; supra-national state, 37; monetary
  integration, 37; common values, 60–1;
  postmodern order, 75, 77–9, 150; post-
  war, 122, 126; differences with US,
  155–72; military capability, 78–9, 156,
  163–4, 168; foreign policy, 160, 169, 171;
  non-military power, 160–1; loss of will to
  power, 165
European Convention on Human Rights,
  132

European Court of Human Rights, 30, 44
European Court of Justice, 30
European Union, 27, 30, 33, 35–44, 50–1, 79,
  107, 111, 122, 139, 147, 168–70;
  constitution, 161; creation of, 57, 134,
  138, 142, 151; imperialism, 71–2, 78–9;
  influence in Balkans, 161; Luxembourg
  compromise, 39; single market, 29

Falkland Islands, 99
fascism, 52–3, 148
financial crises, 70–1
First World War, viii, 4, 43, 65, 90–1, 102,
  133; Arabs in, 97; aftermath, 111, 122, 144
Flanders, 138, 146
foreign policy: coercion, 121, 122; defence
  assistance, 117; and domestic policy, 27,
  29, 102–13, 114, 150, 151, 171; ethical
  dimension, 136–7; European, 160, 169,
  171; exercise of, 113–27; financial
  assistance, 116, 121–4, 126; force, 119–24,
  125–6; national identity and, 130, 132,
  136, 141, 143–7, 149–50; and national
  interests, 127–38, 141, 146, 149–50; peace
  as goal, 111; persuasion, 116, 121–4;
  sanctions, 118–19, 138; US, 170; widening
  the context, 138–51
France, viii, 32, 39, 64, 123, 136, 138; post-
  war, 34, 134, 142–4, 146, 150, 151;
  wartime, 91, 133; Alsace-Lorraine, 140–1,
  144; military spending, 158
Franco, General Francisco, 135
Franco-Prussian War, 144
Franz Ferdinand, Archduke, assassination
  of, 90
free trade, 39, 141

Germany, viii, ix, 12, 24, 40, 123, 131–2;
  unification, 10, 140; post-war, 16, 48, 109,
  121, 134–6, 142–4, 146, 150, 151, 160;
  reunification, 32, 35, 96; strategic
  position, 34–5; Nazi, 52, 128, 133;
  outbreak of World Wars, 91, 95, 101;
  elections, 103; annexation of Alsace-
  Lorraine, 120, 140–1; military forces, 156,
  158, 166; military spending, 158
Gibraltar, 30, 105
Giscard d'Estaing, Valéry, 161
Gladstone, William Ewart, 111
globalization, x, xi, 6, 49, 55, 83, 86, 110
Gorbachev, Mikhail, 98, 108, 124, 145, 159
Grand Alliance, 141
Greece, 108, 158; military spending, 158, 168
Grey, Lord, 91
Guantanamo Bay, 163
Gulf War I, 5, 56–8, 59, 62, 114, 120
Gulf War II, 62, 121, 163

177

INDEX

Hegel, Georg Wilhelm Friedrich, 103
hegemony, 48–9, 58, 65, 69, 76, 77, 83–4,
    108, 163
history, 48, 85
Hitler, Adolf, 55, 94–6, 102, 122, 133, 149
Hobbes, Thomas, 8, 67, 74, 85
Holocaust, 61
Hong Kong, 106
House Committee on un-American
    activities, 93
Hugo, Victor, 7
human rights, 42, 76, 108, 116
Hundred Years' War, vii
Huntington, Samuel, 85
Hussein, Saddam, 26, 48, 56, 98, 121, 122

immigration, illegal, 110
Imperial Preference, 141
imperialism, 25, 32, 42, 69; voluntary, 71–2
India, 24, 43, 57, 77, 144, 162; nuclear
    strategy, 23–4, 31, 62, 128
individuals, freedom of, 76
Indo-China, 141
Indonesia, 19, 20
Industrial Revolution, 10–11, 52
International Atomic Energy Agency
    (IAEA), 31
International Criminal Court, 27, 31; US
    rejection of, 46
international law, 58, 60
International Monetary Fund (IMF), 31, 42,
    43, 70–1, 108, 116, 134
international relations, theories of, 23
internationalism, 76
intervention, 59–61, 68, 73–4, 78, 109, 112
Iran, 98, 106, 108, 129
Iran–Iraq War, 22, 129
Iraq, 50, 56–7, 62, 79, 156, 159, 161, 166;
    post-war, 109, 115, 121; sanctions, 118
Ireland, 33; 'Irish Problem', 144; military
    spending, 158
Iron Curtain, 3
Islam, 25
Israel, 18, 31, 121, 124, 129, 144; US support
    for, 118, 129
Italy, 32, 158; military spending, 158

Japan, 24, 38, 41, 48, 69; security treaty with
    US, 41, 47; post-war, 94, 121, 122, 135,
    141
justice, 164

Kagan, Robert, 156, 159, 162, 164, 169
Kant, Immanuel, 7, 40, 74
Karzai, Hamid, 123
Kashmir, 83
Kennan, George, 99, 125, 170

Kennedy, John F., 84, 89, 96, 127–8
Khrushchev, Nikita, 89
Kissinger, Henry, 60, 76, 79, 99; quoted 150
Korea, 13, 48, 49, 83, 92–3, 99, 109, 141;
    Japanese occupation, 120
Korean War, 91–2
Kosovo, 59, 61, 71, 106, 120, 123, 144, 156,
    161
Kostunica, Vojislav, 147
Kristol, Irving, 150
Kuwait, 26, 56, 58, 99

land-mines 104
Latin America, see South America
League of Nations, 5, 58, 111, 168
Lebanon, 120
Lenin, Vladimir Ilyich, 117
liberalism, 14, 51
Liberia, 16, 66
Libya, 115
linkage, 138
Lockerbie bombing, 119
Logue, Christopher, quoted, 152

MacArthur, General, 91
Macartney, Lord, 88–9, 107
Macedonia, 109
Machiavelli, Niccolò, 10, 20, 22, 31, 120
Macmillan, Harold, 96, 127–8
Mao Zedong, 124
Marshall Plan, 126, 134
Masood, Ahmed, 68
McCloy, General, 143
McNamara, Robert, 93, 99, 127
Melos, 131
MERCOSUR, 42
Metternich, Prince, 11, 132
Mexico, 51
Milosevic, Slobodan, 59, 95, 96, 118, 120, 147
Mitchell, Senator, 114
modern world, 21–6, 29, 39–40, 56, 76–7
Mogul Empire, 18
Monnet, Jean, 138, 142, 145, 151
Monroe Doctrine, 12, 47
multilateralism, 164, 168, 170
Mutiny Acts, 9

NAFTA, 42
Napoleon Bonaparte, 121, 143, 149, 167
Nasser, Gamal Abd al-, 5, 97, 124
nation states, 5–6, 19, 21, 22, 24, 26, 59,
    68–70, 72
national identity, 20–1, 32, 70, 87, 130, 132,
    136, 141, 143–4; common, 146–7, 149–50,
    171; multiple, 51
national interests, 23, 87, 141; hollowness of,
    38–40, 50–54, 127–38, 146–7, 149–50

INDEX

nationalism, 7, 14, 26, 52, 61, 70, 76, 93
NATO, 33, 35, 39–40, 47, 57, 61, 79, 111,
123, 143, 161, 166
neoconservatives, 49
Netherlands, 137; military spending, 158
neutrality, 137
new world order, 55, 57, 58, 74, 75
Nicaragua, 13
Nietzsche, Friedrich, 164
Nixon, Richard M., 50
non-governmental organizations (NGOs),
104
Non-Proliferation Treaty (NPT), 31
nuclear weapons, 13, 32, 34, 38, 46, 62–5, 77,
83, 125–30, 131, 161; proliferation, 63–4

Occupied Territories, 18, 105, 121
oil supplies, 38, 56
Opium Wars, 89
Organization for Economic Co-operation
and Development (OECD), 31, 143
Organization for Security and Co-operation
in Europe (OSCE), 26, 29, 38, 41
Oslo process, 114
Ottawa Convention, 27
Ottoman Empire, 18, 20, 70, 72

Pacific, 22, 26, 122
pacifism, 111, 137
Pakistan, 23, 31, 62, 66, 68, 128, 144
Palestine, 105, 114, 124, 129, 144
Palestinian Authority, 109
Palmerston, Lord, 22, 38, 39
Parsons, Sir Anthony, 99–100
Pax Americana, 49
Pax Britannica, 49
Pax Romana, 49
Paz, Octavio, 48
peace, 111, 149
Perkovich, George, 128
Persian Empire, 68
Persian Gulf, 22, 23, 26
Peyrefitte, Alain, 89
Poland, 54, 95, 109, 131; British guarantee,
133
Polaris, 127
policing, 44
Portugal, 20, 21, 108; military spending, 158
postmodern world, 26–44, 47, 50, 53–4, 71,
73–4, 171; intervention, 59–60; security,
31–2, 50, 75–80, 161
pre-modern world, 16–18, 24, 25, 32, 59, 76;
chaos, 65–75, 77
privatization, 51, 108
prostitution, 67
race, 25, 70
raison d'état, 10, 22, 31, 53, 79

Rapid Reaction Force, 156
Reagan, Ronald, 98
refugees, 66, 67
regime change, 46, 109, 148
religion, 18–21; wars of, 21
revolutions, 3
Rhodesia, 119
Richelieu, Cardinal, 143
Roman Empire, 70, 78
Rome, fall of, 68
Rome, Treaty of, 26
Roosevelt, Franklin D., 95, 96, 100, 141, 148,
165
Russia, 34, 35, 95, 123; treaties, 30, 47;
problems with, 41, 146; foreign policy, 54;
outbreak of First World War, 90–1, 102,
107; 'evil empire', 98; border disputes,
139; change in identity, 149
Russian Empire, 18, 20
Rwanda, 66, 67

Saint-Simon, Comte de, 7
Salvation Army, 90
sanctions, 118–19, 138
Saragossa, Treaty of, 21
Sarajevo, 90
Saudi Arabia, 48, 56
Saxony, 145
Scotland, 24, 145
Second World War, 4, 11, 12, 16, 61, 101;
aftermath, 111, 115, 120, 122, 126, 133,
135, 165
security, x, 5, 43, 44–6, 51, 53, 55, 65, 74, 151,
163; collective, 57–8; postmodern, 31–2,
50, 75–80, 161
Serbia, 59, 90, 107; sanctions, 118, 119
Seven Years' War, 11
Shakespeare, William: *Hamlet*, quoted, 55;
Troilus and Cressida, quoted, 173
Sierra Leone, 66, 67, 147
slave trade, 132
Slovenia, 122
Somalia, 16, 66, 73, 75, 147
South Africa, 119
South America (Latin America), 12, 17, 42
Soviet empire, 19, 20
Soviet Union, x, 10, 13, 17, 53–4, 95, 98, 99,
100, 108, 121, 124, 134; break-up, 14, 129;
dealings with West, 148, 159; gas pipeline,
159
Spain, 21, 64, 108, 135, 158; Gibraltar
dispute, 30, 105; military spending, 158
Srebrenica, 84
Sri Lanka, 144
Stalin, Joseph, 95–6, 100, 134, 148
START Treaty, 47
states, 10, 16–18, 20, 21, 23–5, 26, 32, 38, 76,